Android Games
Design Patterns

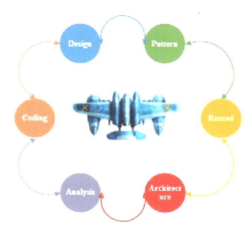

YANG HU

Simple is the beginning of wisdom. This book briefly explain the concept and real practice examples in games, you will learn easy and fun.

http://en.verejava.com

CONTENTS

If you want to learn this book, you must have basic knowledge of Java, you can learn book: << Easy Learning Java(2 Edition)>>

https://www.amazon.com/dp/B086VLLTGK

If you already have basic knowledge of Java, skip it, start an exciting journey

Download MobileGameDesignPatternImages.zip all images for this book.
http://en.verejava.com/download.jsp?id=1

Android Studio Installation

1. Graphic installation steps please click below link:

http://en.verejava.com/?id=2321332638911

Create Android Game Project

1. Open Android Studio File -> New -> New Project

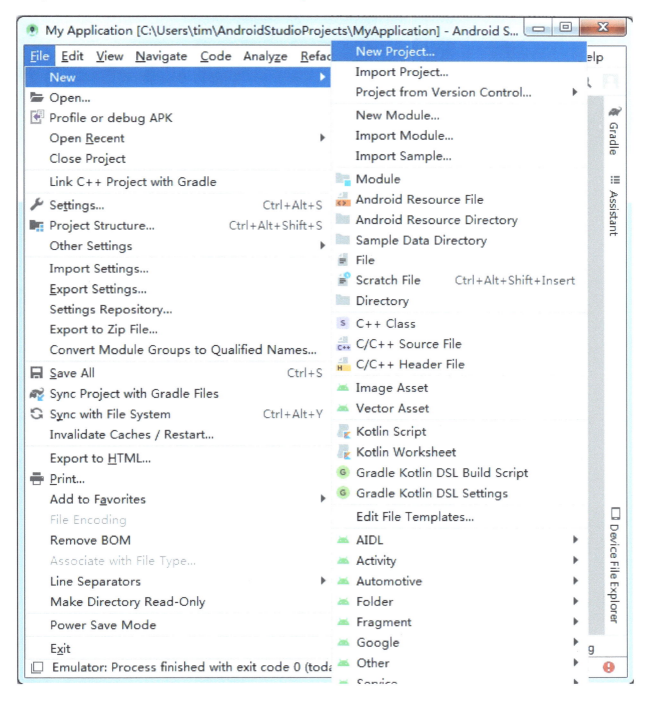

2. Select Empty Activity and then Click Next Button

Activity: An Android activity is one screen of the Android app's user interface. In that way an Android activity
is very similar to windows in a desktop application. An Android app may contain one or more activities,
meaning one or more screens.

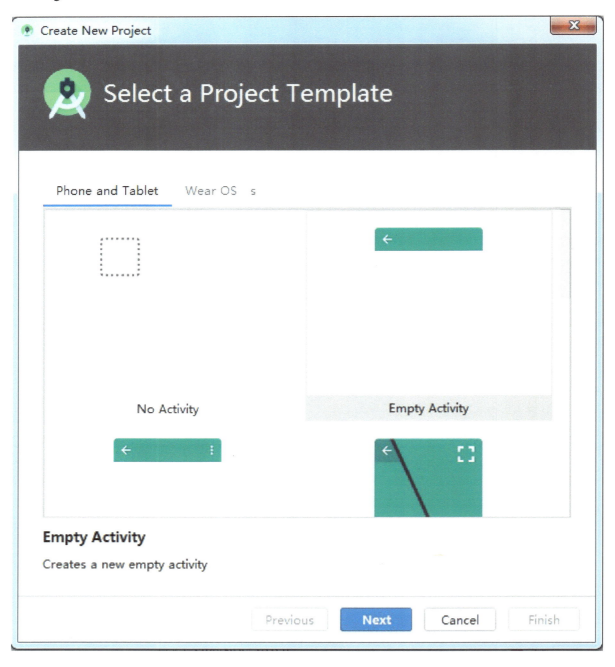

3. Input Project information and then Click Finish Button

Name: Project Name
Package name: The package name is a unique name to identify a specific app.
Save location: Project location
Language: Java

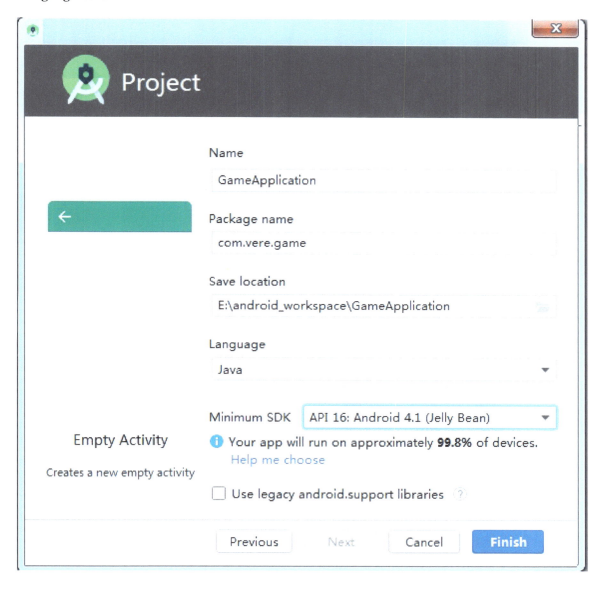

4. Select The New Device 1 API 22 And then Click Green Arrow Button Run

New Device 1 API 22 ▼   ▶

setContentView(R.layout.*activity_main*): Set the activity content from a layout resource. It can be a view or an xml layout file.

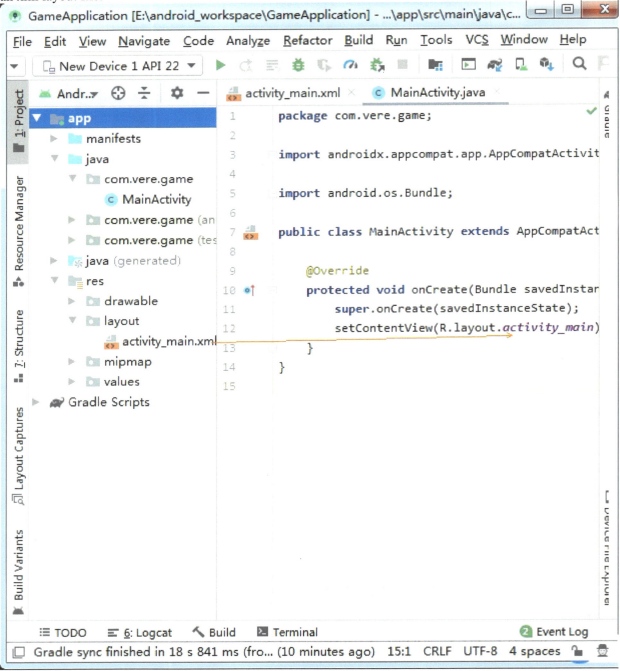

5. Very excited, you will see the first Android program in the phone simulator

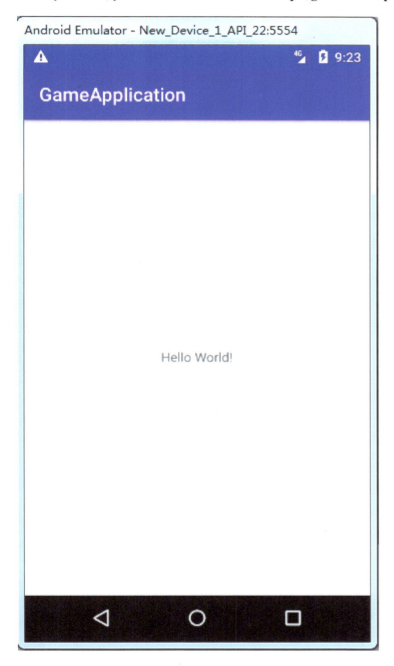

Create GameView

1. Create a GameView to inherit SurfaceView
2. SurfaceView are provides a drawing surface embedded inside of View hierarchy.
3. GameView implements SurfaceHolder.Callback interface to receive information about changes to the surface.
4. GameView implements Runnable for game loop to repeat drawGame(Canvas canvas).
5. Draw a BluePlane Bitmap on canvas in method drawGame(Canvas canvas).
6. MainActivity set GameView as View by setContentView(new GameView(this))

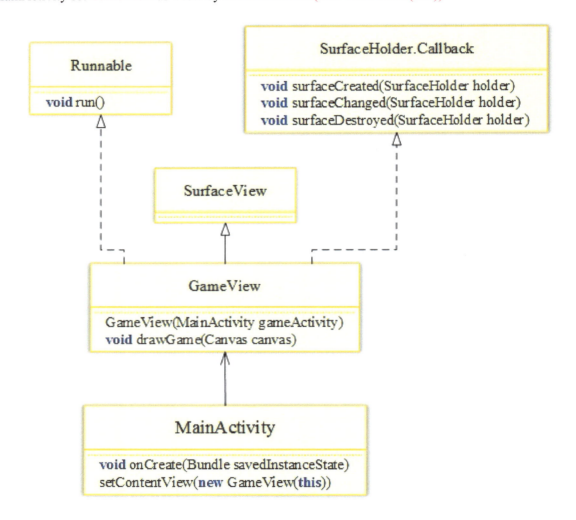

Draw a BluePlane Bitmap on canvas in method drawGame(Canvas canvas).
x, y coordinates:

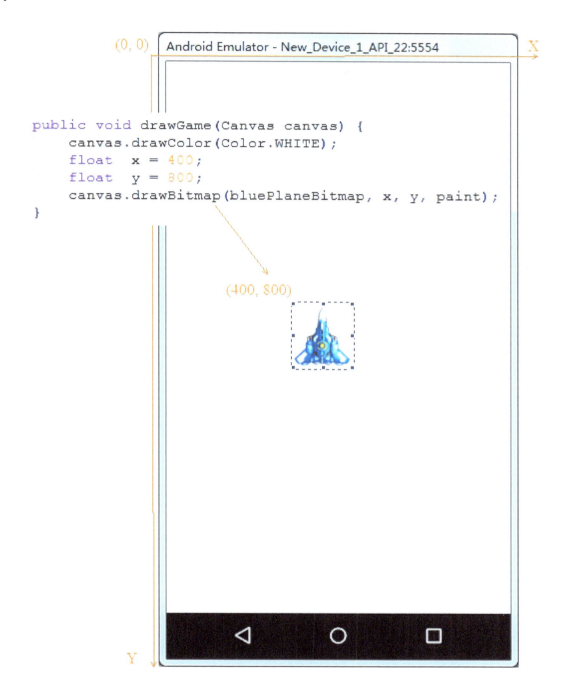

```
public void drawGame(Canvas canvas) {
    canvas.drawColor(Color.WHITE);
    float  x = 400;
    float  y = 800;
    canvas.drawBitmap(bluePlaneBitmap, x, y, paint);
}
```

1. Create a GameView

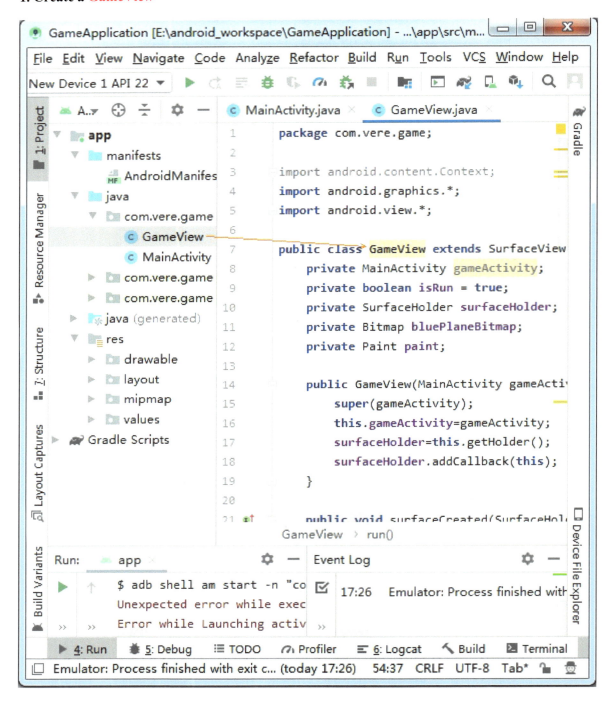

2. Copy blue_plane.png to res -> drawable

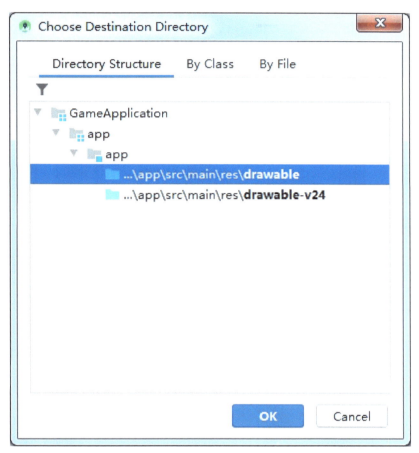

Click Ok Button

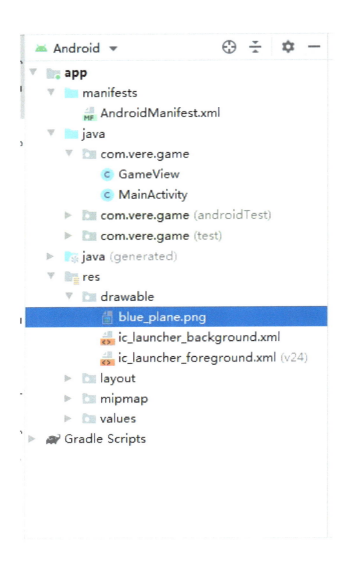

3. GameView.java:

```java
package com.vere.game;
import android.content.Context;
import android.graphics.*;
import android.view.*;

public class GameView extends SurfaceView implements Runnable , SurfaceHolder.Callback {
    private MainActivity gameActivity;
    private boolean isRun = true; // for game loop
    private SurfaceHolder surfaceHolder;
    private Bitmap bluePlaneBitmap; // blue_plane.png image bitmap
    private Paint paint;

    public GameView(MainActivity gameActivity) {
        super(gameActivity);
        this.gameActivity=gameActivity;
        surfaceHolder=this.getHolder();
        surfaceHolder.addCallback(this);
    }

    //called immediately after the surface is first created
    public void surfaceCreated(SurfaceHolder holder){
        this.surfaceHolder=holder;
        paint=new Paint();
        //read bitmap resource res -> drawable -> blue_plane.png
        bluePlaneBitmap= BitmapFactory.decodeResource(getResources(), R.drawable.blue_plane);

        new Thread(this).start(); // start game loop thread
    }

    //called immediately after any structural changes.
    public void surfaceChanged(SurfaceHolder holder, int format, int width,int height){

    }

    //called immediately before a surface is being destroyed.
    public void surfaceDestroyed(SurfaceHolder holder){
        isRun = false;
    }

    public void drawGame(Canvas canvas) {
        canvas.drawColor(Color.WHITE); //set white background
        float  x = 400; //x coordinate
        float  y = 800; //y coordinate
        canvas.drawBitmap(bluePlaneBitmap, x, y, paint); // draw image on canvas
    }
```

```
// game loop to repeat draw graphics and images
public void run(){
    while(isRun){
        Canvas canvas=null;
        try{
            canvas=surfaceHolder.lockCanvas(); // lock canvas
            synchronized (surfaceHolder){
                drawGame(canvas); // draw images of games
            }
            Thread.sleep(100); // sleep 100 ms
        } catch (Exception e){
            e.printStackTrace();
        }
        finally{
            if(canvas!=null){
                //unlock canvas submit
                surfaceHolder.unlockCanvasAndPost(canvas);
            }
        }
    }
}
```

4. MainActivity.java set GameView as View by setContentView(new GameView(this))

```
package com.vere.game;

import androidx.appcompat.app.AppCompatActivity;
import android.os.Bundle;
import android.view.*;

public class MainActivity extends AppCompatActivity {

    @Override
    protected void onCreate(Bundle savedInstanceState) {
        //Set MainActivity full-screen and no title bar
        supportRequestWindowFeature(Window.FEATURE_NO_TITLE);
        getWindow().setFlags(WindowManager.LayoutParams.FLAG_FULLSCREEN,
WindowManager.LayoutParams.FLAG_FULLSCREEN);
        super.onCreate(savedInstanceState);
        setContentView(new GameView(this));
    }
}
```

5. Select The New Device 1 API 22 And then Click Green Arrow Button Run

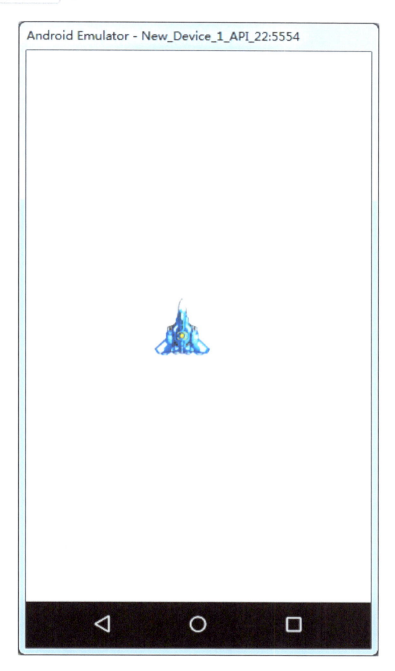

Template Pattern Game

Template Pattern: Defer the exact steps of an algorithm to a subclass. Define the skeleton of an algorithm in an operation, deferring some steps to subclasses. Template Method lets subclasses redefine certain steps of an algorithm without changing the algorithm's structure.

1. **BluePlane inherit from Sprite Template for reuse.**

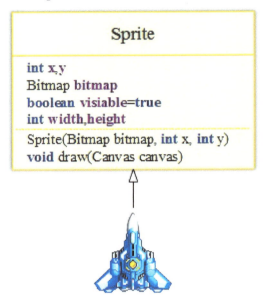

2. **BluePlane draw on bottom center of canvas in GameView.**

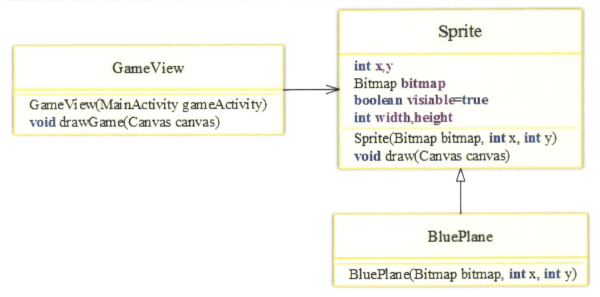

Android Emulator - New_Device_1_API_22:5554

canvasHeight

```java
public void surfaceCreated(SurfaceHolder holder) {
    this.canvasWidth = this.getWidth(); // get width of canvas
    this.canvasHeight = this.getHeight(); // get height of canvas
    this.surfaceHolder = holder;
    paint = new Paint();

    //draw blue plane on bottom center of canvas
    bluePlaneBitmap = BitmapFactory.decodeResource(getResources(),
            R.drawable.blue_plane);
    bluePlane = new BluePlane(bluePlaneBitmap,  x: 0,   y: 0);
    bluePlane.setX(this.canvasWidth/2 - bluePlane.getWidth()/2);
    bluePlane.setY(this.canvasHeight - bluePlane.getHeight() - 40);

    new Thread( target: this).start(); // start game loop thread
}
```

Sprite:

1. **x:** x coordinate of Canvas
2. **y:** y coordinate of Canvas
3. **Bitmap bitmap:** the image of BluePlane (blue_plane.png)
4. **boolean visiable=true:** if visiable=true can show on canvas.
5. **int width,height:** the width and height of canvas

Sprite.java

```java
package com.vere.game;
import android.graphics.*;

public abstract class Sprite {
    protected int x,y;//Sprite x, y coordinates
    protected Bitmap bitmap;//Pictures of sprite
    protected boolean visiable=true;//Is the sprite visible
    protected int width,height;//Sprite width and height

    public Sprite(Bitmap bitmap, int x, int y) {
        super();
        this.bitmap = bitmap;
        this.width=bitmap.getWidth();
        this.height=bitmap.getHeight();
        this.x = x;
        this.y = y;
    }

    //draw sprite on canvas
    public void draw(Canvas canvas){
        if(this.isVisiable()){
            canvas.drawBitmap(this.bitmap, this.x, this.y, null);
        }
    }

    public int getX(){
        return x;
    }
    public void setX(int x){
        this.x = x;
    }

    public int getY(){
        return y;
    }

    public void setY(int y){
        this.y = y;
    }
```

```java
   public boolean isVisiable(){
      return visiable;
   }
   public void setVisiable(boolean visiable){
      this.visiable = visiable;
   }

   public void setWidth(int width) {
      this.width = width;
   }
   public int getWidth() {
      return this.width;
   }

   public void setHeight(int height){
      this.height = height;
   }
   public int getHeight(){
      return this.height;
   }
}
```

BluePlane.java

```java
package com.vere.game;

import android.graphics.Bitmap;

public class BluePlane extends Sprite {

   public BluePlane(Bitmap bitmap, int x, int y) {
      super(bitmap, x, y);
   }
}
```

GameView.java

```java
package com.vere.game;
import android.content.Context;
import android.graphics.*;
import android.view.*;

public class GameView extends SurfaceView implements Runnable, SurfaceHolder.Callback {
    private MainActivity gameActivity;
    private boolean isRun = true;
    private SurfaceHolder surfaceHolder;
    private Bitmap bluePlaneBitmap;
    private Paint paint;
    private Sprite bluePlane;
    private int canvasWidth, canvasHeight;

    public GameView(MainActivity gameActivity) {
        super(gameActivity);
        this.gameActivity = gameActivity;
        surfaceHolder = this.getHolder();
        surfaceHolder.addCallback(this);
    }

    public void surfaceCreated(SurfaceHolder holder) {
        this.canvasWidth = this.getWidth(); // get width of canvas
        this.canvasHeight = this.getHeight(); // get height of canvas
        this.surfaceHolder = holder;
        paint = new Paint();

        //draw blue plane on bottom center of canvas
        bluePlaneBitmap = BitmapFactory.decodeResource(getResources(), R.drawable.blue_plane);
        bluePlane = new BluePlane(bluePlaneBitmap, 0, 0);
        bluePlane.setX(this.canvasWidth/2 - bluePlane.getWidth()/2);
        bluePlane.setY(this.canvasHeight - bluePlane.getHeight() - 40);

        new Thread(this).start(); // start game loop thread
    }

    public void surfaceChanged(SurfaceHolder holder, int format, int width, int height) {

    }

    public void surfaceDestroyed(SurfaceHolder holder) {
        isRun = false;
    }
```

```java
public void drawGame(Canvas canvas) {
    canvas.drawColor(Color.WHITE);
    bluePlane.draw(canvas); //draw plane on canvas
}

// game loop to repeat draw
public void run() {
    while (isRun) {
        Canvas canvas = null;
        try {
            canvas = surfaceHolder.lockCanvas();
            synchronized (surfaceHolder) {
                drawGame(canvas); // draw images of games
            }
            Thread.sleep(100);
        } catch (Exception e) {
            e.printStackTrace();
        } finally {
            if (canvas != null) {
                surfaceHolder.unlockCanvasAndPost(canvas);
            }
        }
    }
}
}
```

MainActivity.java

```java
package com.vere.game;

import androidx.appcompat.app.AppCompatActivity;
import android.os.Bundle;
import android.view.*;

public class MainActivity extends AppCompatActivity {

    @Override
    protected void onCreate(Bundle savedInstanceState) {
        supportRequestWindowFeature(Window.FEATURE_NO_TITLE);
        getWindow().setFlags(WindowManager.LayoutParams.FLAG_FULLSCREEN,
WindowManager.LayoutParams.FLAG_FULLSCREEN);
        super.onCreate(savedInstanceState);
        setContentView(new GameView(this));
    }
}
```

5. Select The New Device 1 API 22 And then Click Green Arrow Button Run

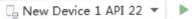

Flyweight Pattern Game

FlyWeight Pattern : A fine-grained instance used for efficient sharing. Use sharing to support large numbers of fine-grained objects efficiently. A flyweight is a shared object that can be used in multiple contexts simultaneously.

ImageCache store game images like(Plane, EnemyPlane,Bullet).
1. ImageCache preload BluePlane in MainActivity.
2. Create BluePlane that image from ImageCache.
3. Mouse click BluePlane and drag to move.

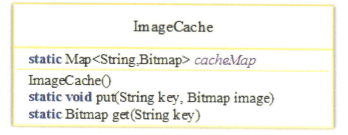

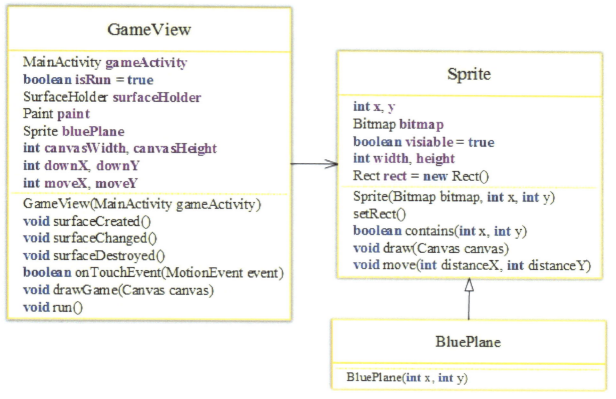

1. The x, y coordinates of the mouse are in the area of BluePlane

```
if (bluePlane.contains(downX, downY)) {
    //The plane follows the mouse move
    bluePlane.move(distanceX, distanceY);
}
```

Android Emulator - New_Device_1_API_22:5554

2. Mouse click and then drag BluePlane to move.

```java
public boolean onTouchEvent(MotionEvent event) {
    if (event.getAction() == MotionEvent.ACTION_DOWN) {
        downX = (int) event.getX();
        downY = (int) event.getY();
    } else if (event.getAction() == MotionEvent.ACTION_MOVE) {
        moveX = (int) event.getX();
        moveY = (int) event.getY();

        //Calculate the distance moved by the mouse
        int distanceX = moveX - downX;
        int distanceY = moveY - downY;

        if (bluePlane.contains(downX, downY)) {
            //The plane follows the mouse move
            bluePlane.move(distanceX, distanceY);
        }

        //Save moving coordinates to down coordinates
        downX = moveX;
        downY = moveY;
    }
    return true;
}
```

25

```java
package com.vere.game;

import android.graphics.*;

public abstract class Sprite {
    protected int x, y;//Sprite x, y coordinates
    protected Bitmap bitmap;//Pictures of sprite
    protected boolean visible = true;//Is the sprite visible
    protected int width, height;//Sprite width and height

    public Sprite(Bitmap bitmap, int x, int y) {
        super();
        this.bitmap = bitmap;
        this.width = bitmap.getWidth();
        this.height = bitmap.getHeight();
        this.x = x;
        this.y = y;
    }

    //if the mouse (x, y) is in area of Sprite
    public boolean contains(int x, int y) {
        if((x - this.x < this.width) && (y - this.y < this.height)){
            return true;
        }
        return false;
    }

    //draw sprite on canvas
    public void draw(Canvas canvas) {
        if (this.isVisible()) {
            canvas.drawBitmap(this.bitmap, this.x, this.y, null);
        }
    }

    //move sprite on canvas
    //distanceX: The distance moved in the x-axis
    //distanceY: The distance moved in the y-axis
    public void move(int distanceX, int distanceY) {
        this.x += distanceX;
        this.y += distanceY;
    }

    public int getX() {
        return x;
    }
```

```java
    public void setX(int x) {
        this.x = x;
    }

    public int getY() {
        return y;
    }

    public void setY(int y) {
        this.y = y;
    }

    public boolean isVisible() {
        return visible;
    }

    public void setVisible(boolean visible) {
        this.visible = visible;
    }

    public void setWidth(int width) {
        this.width = width;
    }

    public int getWidth() {
        return this.width;
    }

    public void setHeight(int height) {
        this.height = height;
    }

    public int getHeight() {
        return this.height;
    }

    public Bitmap getBitmap() {
        return bitmap;
    }

    public void setBitmap(Bitmap bitmap) {
        this.bitmap = bitmap;
    }
}
```

ImageCache.java

```java
package com.vere.game;

import android.graphics.Bitmap;
import java.util.*;

public class ImageCache {
    private static Map<String,Bitmap> cacheMap=new HashMap<String, Bitmap>();

    private ImageCache(){}

    public static void put(String key, Bitmap image){
        cacheMap.put(key, image);
    }

    public static Bitmap get(String key){
        return cacheMap.get(key);
    }
}
```

BluePlane.java

```java
package com.vere.game;

import android.graphics.Bitmap;

public class BluePlane extends Sprite {

    public BluePlane(int x, int y) {
        super(ImageCache.get("bluePlaneBitmap"), x, y);
    }
}
```

GameView.java

```java
package com.vere.game;
import android.content.Context;
import android.graphics.*;
import android.view.*;

public class GameView extends SurfaceView implements Runnable, SurfaceHolder.Callback {
    private MainActivity gameActivity;
    private boolean isRun = true;
    private SurfaceHolder surfaceHolder;
    private Paint paint;
    private Sprite bluePlane;
    private int canvasWidth, canvasHeight;
    private int downX, downY;//coordinates of the mouse down
    private int moveX, moveY;//coordinates of the mouse move

    public GameView(MainActivity gameActivity) {
        super(gameActivity);
        this.gameActivity = gameActivity;

        surfaceHolder = this.getHolder();
        surfaceHolder.addCallback(this);
    }

    public void surfaceCreated(SurfaceHolder holder) {
        this.setFocusable(true);
        this.setFocusableInTouchMode(true);
        this.canvasWidth = this.getWidth(); // get width of canvas
        this.canvasHeight = this.getHeight(); // get height of canvas
        this.surfaceHolder = holder;
        paint = new Paint();

        //draw blue plane on bottom center of canvas
        bluePlane = new BluePlane(0, 0);
        bluePlane.setX(this.canvasWidth / 2 - bluePlane.getWidth() / 2);
        bluePlane.setY(this.canvasHeight - bluePlane.getHeight() - 40);

        new Thread(this).start(); // start game loop thread
    }

    public void surfaceChanged(SurfaceHolder holder, int format, int width, int height) {

    }

    public void surfaceDestroyed(SurfaceHolder holder) {
        isRun = false;
    }
```

29

```java
public boolean onTouchEvent(MotionEvent event) {
    if (event.getAction() == MotionEvent.ACTION_DOWN) {
        downX = (int) event.getX();
        downY = (int) event.getY();
    } else if (event.getAction() == MotionEvent.ACTION_MOVE) {
        moveX = (int) event.getX();
        moveY = (int) event.getY();

        //Calculate the distance moved by the mouse
        int distanceX = moveX - downX;
        int distanceY = moveY - downY;

        if (bluePlane.contains(downX, downY)) {
            //The plane follows the mouse move
            bluePlane.move(distanceX, distanceY);
        }

        //Save moving coordinates to down coordinates
        downX = moveX;
        downY = moveY;
    }
    return true;
}

public void drawGame(Canvas canvas) {
    canvas.drawColor(Color.WHITE);
    bluePlane.draw(canvas); //draw plane on canvas
}

public void run() {
    while (isRun) {
        Canvas canvas = null;
        try {
            canvas = surfaceHolder.lockCanvas();
            synchronized (surfaceHolder) {
                drawGame(canvas); // draw images of games
            }
            Thread.sleep(50);
        } catch (Exception e) {
            e.printStackTrace();
        } finally {
            if (canvas != null) {
                surfaceHolder.unlockCanvasAndPost(canvas);
            }
        }
    }
}
}
```

MainActivity.java

```java
package com.vere.game;

import androidx.appcompat.app.AppCompatActivity;

import android.graphics.Bitmap;
import android.graphics.BitmapFactory;
import android.os.Bundle;
import android.view.*;

public class MainActivity extends AppCompatActivity {

    @Override
    protected void onCreate(Bundle savedInstanceState) {
        supportRequestWindowFeature(Window.FEATURE_NO_TITLE);
        getWindow().setFlags(WindowManager.LayoutParams.FLAG_FULLSCREEN,
WindowManager.LayoutParams.FLAG_FULLSCREEN);
        super.onCreate(savedInstanceState);

        Bitmap bluePlaneBitmap = BitmapFactory.decodeResource(getResources(), R.drawable.blue_plane);
        ImageCache.put("bluePlaneBitmap", bluePlaneBitmap);

        setContentView(new GameView(this));
    }
}
```

Builder Pattern Game

Builder Pattern: Separates object construction from its representation. Separate the construction of a complex object from its representation so that the same construction processes can create different representations.

1. load res->layout->select_plane.xml as planeSelectView.
2. Create AlertDialog by AlertDialog.Builder.
3. dialog setContentView(planeSelectView).
4. Builder create dialog to show

UML Diagram

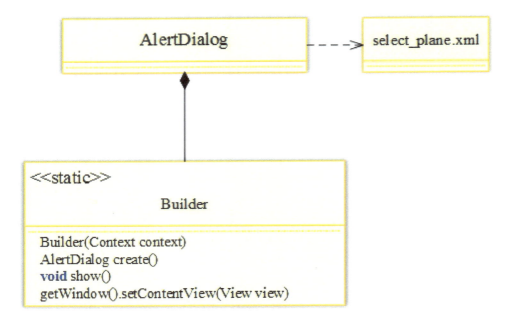

1. Create Layout res->layout->select_plane.xml.

```
app
  manifests
  java
  ▶ com.vere.game
  ▶ com.vere.game (andro
  ▶ com.vere.game (test)
  java (generated)
  res
  ▼ drawable
      blue_plane.png
      blue_plane_big.png
      ic_launcher_backgro
      ic_launcher_foregro
      red_plane_big.png
  ▼ layout
      activity_main.xml
      select_plane.xml
  ▶ mipmap
  ▶ values
  Gradle Scripts
```

```xml
7      tools:context=".MainActivity">                          ❶
8
9      <LinearLayout
10         android:layout_width="fill_parent"
11         android:layout_height="wrap_content"
12         android:orientation="horizontal"
13         android:layout_gravity="center_horizontal"
14         tools:layout_editor_absoluteX="1dp"
15         tools:layout_editor_absoluteY="1dp">
16
17         <ImageView
18             android:id="@+id/bluePlane"
19             android:layout_width="wrap_content"
20             android:layout_height="wrap_content"
21             android:layout_weight="1"
22             android:layout_gravity="center_horizontal"
23             app:srcCompat="@drawable/blue_plane_big" />
24
25         <ImageView
26             android:id="@+id/redPlane"
27             android:layout_width="wrap_content"
28             android:layout_height="wrap_content"
29             android:layout_weight="1"
30             android:layout_gravity="center_horizontal"
31             app:srcCompat="@drawable/red_plane_big" />
32     </LinearLayout>
33     <droidx.constraintlayout.widget.ConstraintLayout>
```

roidx.constraintlayout.widget.ConstraintLayout > LinearLayout

```
17      <ImageView
18          android:id="@+id/bluePlane"
19          android:layout_width="wrap_content"
20          android:layout_height="wrap_content"
21          android:layout_weight="1"
22          android:layout_gravity="center_horizontal"
23          app:srcCompat="@drawable/blue_plane_big" />

25      <ImageView
26          android:id="@+id/redPlane"
27          android:layout_width="wrap_content"
28          android:layout_height="wrap_content"
29          android:layout_weight="1"
30          android:layout_gravity="center_horizontal"
31          app:srcCompat="@drawable/red_plane_big" />
32  </LinearLayout>
33  <droidx constraintlayout widget ConstraintLayout>
```

roidx.constraintlayout.widget.ConstraintLayout > LinearLayout

  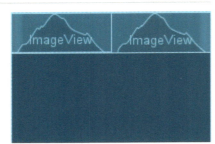

MainActivity.java

```java
package com.vere.game;

import androidx.appcompat.app.AppCompatActivity;

import android.app.AlertDialog;
import android.graphics.Bitmap;
import android.graphics.BitmapFactory;
import android.os.Bundle;
import android.view.*;
import android.widget.ImageView;

public class MainActivity extends AppCompatActivity {

    private AlertDialog dialog;

    @Override
    protected void onCreate(Bundle savedInstanceState) {
        supportRequestWindowFeature(Window.FEATURE_NO_TITLE);
        getWindow().setFlags(WindowManager.LayoutParams.FLAG_FULLSCREEN,
WindowManager.LayoutParams.FLAG_FULLSCREEN);
        super.onCreate(savedInstanceState);

        //AlertDialog
        AlertDialog.Builder builder=new AlertDialog.Builder(this);

        //load res->layout->select_plane.xml
        View planeSelectView=View.inflate(this, R.layout.select_plane, null);
        //get ImageView Object
        ImageView btnBluePlane=(ImageView)planeSelectView.findViewById(R.id.bluePlane);
        ImageView btnRedPlane=(ImageView)planeSelectView.findViewById(R.id.redPlane);

        //build a dialog
        dialog=builder.create();
        //show dialog
        dialog.show();

        //replace dialog content view
        dialog.getWindow().setContentView(planeSelectView);
    }
}
```

Select The New Device 1 API 22 And then Click Green Arrow Button Run

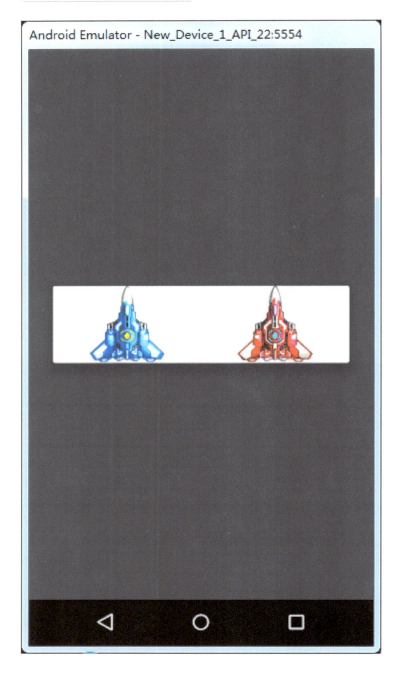

Command Pattern Game

Command Pattern :

Encapsulate a request as an object, allowing you to parameterize different requests.

1. Create AlertDialog
2. BluePlaneImageView and RedPlaneImageView setOnClickListener
3. Mouse click BluePlaneImageView or RedPlaneImageView.
   the void onClick(View v) will be called automatically.
4. Close AlertDialog.

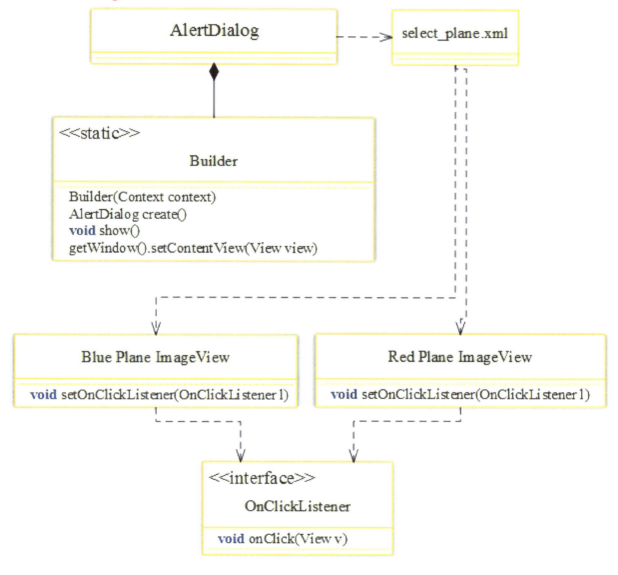

MainActivity.java

```java
package com.vere.game;

import androidx.appcompat.app.AppCompatActivity;

import android.app.AlertDialog;
import android.content.DialogInterface;
import android.graphics.Bitmap;
import android.graphics.BitmapFactory;
import android.os.Bundle;
import android.view.*;
import android.widget.ImageView;
import android.widget.Toast;

public class MainActivity extends AppCompatActivity {

    private AlertDialog dialog;

    @Override
    protected void onCreate(Bundle savedInstanceState) {
        supportRequestWindowFeature(Window.FEATURE_NO_TITLE);
        getWindow().setFlags(WindowManager.LayoutParams.FLAG_FULLSCREEN,
WindowManager.LayoutParams.FLAG_FULLSCREEN);
        super.onCreate(savedInstanceState);

        //AlertDialog
        AlertDialog.Builder builder=new AlertDialog.Builder(this);

        //load res->layout->select_plane.xml
        View planeSelectView=View.inflate(this, R.layout.select_plane, null);
        //get ImageView Object
        ImageView btnBluePlane=(ImageView)planeSelectView.findViewById(R.id.bluePlane);
        ImageView btnRedPlane=(ImageView)planeSelectView.findViewById(R.id.redPlane);

        //Set click command event
        btnBluePlane.setOnClickListener(new View.OnClickListener()
        {
            public void onClick(View v)
            {
                Toast.makeText(MainActivity.this, "BluePlane is selected", Toast.LENGTH_SHORT).show();
                dialog.dismiss();

            }
        });
```

```java
    btnRedPlane.setOnClickListener(new View.OnClickListener()
    {
      public void onClick(View v)
      {
        Toast.makeText(MainActivity.this, "RedPlane is selected", Toast.LENGTH_SHORT).show();
        dialog.dismiss();

      }
    });

    //build a dialog
    dialog=builder.create();
    //show dialog
    dialog.show();

    //replace dialog content view
    dialog.getWindow().setContentView(planeSelectView);

  }
}
```

Select The New Device 1 API 22 And then Click Green Arrow Button Run

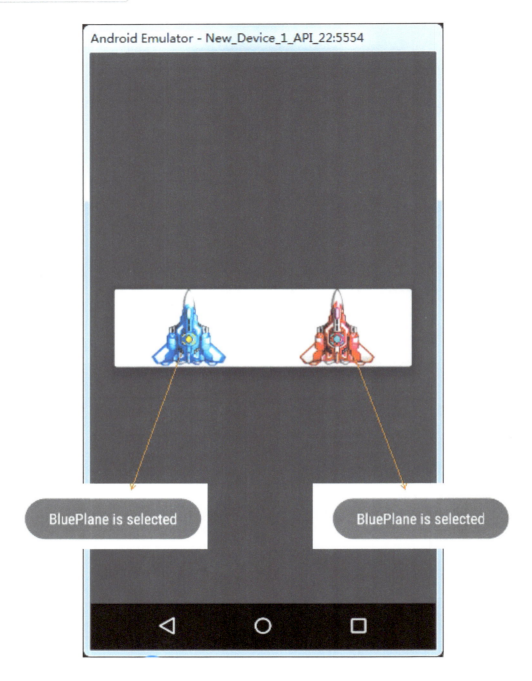

Factory Pattern Game

Factory Pattern: Creates an instance of several derived classes. Define an interface for creating an object, but let subclasses decide which class to instantiate. Factory Method lets a class defer instantiation to subclasses.

1. BluePlane and RedPlane can be created by the SpriteFactory

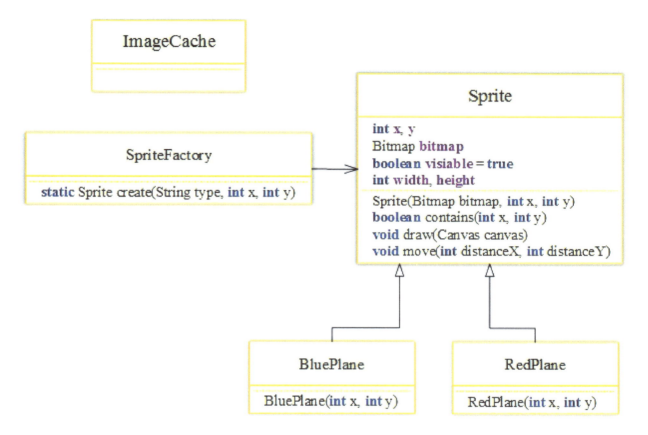

Select BluePlane and RedPlane setContentView by GameView
Pass parameters to GameView if planeType = "1": BluePlane, if planeType="2": RedPlane

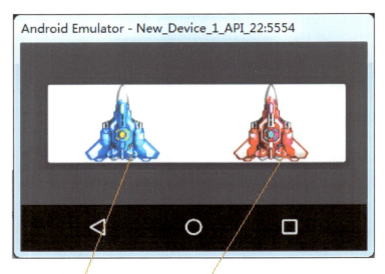

```
//Set click command event
btnBluePlane.setOnClickListener(new View.OnClickListener()
{
    public void onClick(View v)
    {
        MainActivity.this.setContentView(new GameView(MainActivity.this,"1"));
        dialog.dismiss();

    }
});
btnRedPlane.setOnClickListener(new View.OnClickListener()
{
    public void onClick(View v)
    {
        MainActivity.this.setContentView(new GameView(MainActivity.this,"2"));
        dialog.dismiss();

    }
});
```

Select BluePlane can be created by the SpriteFactory draw on canvas

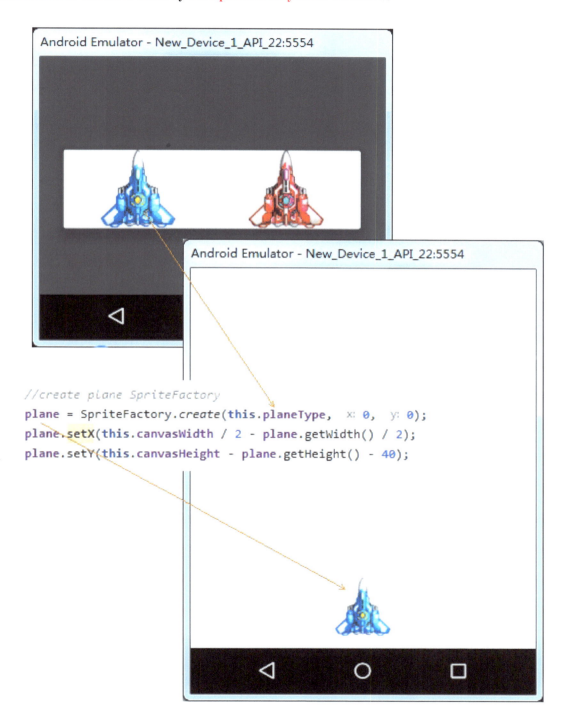

```
//create plane SpriteFactory
plane = SpriteFactory.create(this.planeType,  x: 0,  y: 0);
plane.setX(this.canvasWidth / 2 - plane.getWidth() / 2);
plane.setY(this.canvasHeight - plane.getHeight() - 40);
```

Select RedPlane can be created by the SpriteFactory draw on canvas

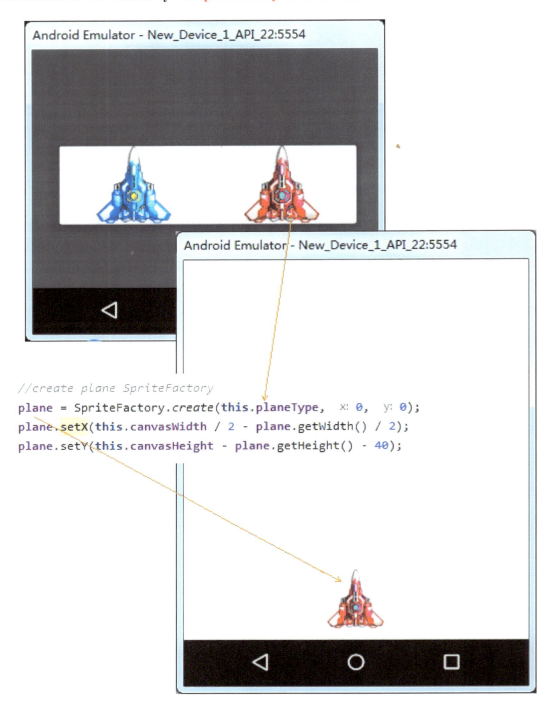

Sprite.java

```java
package com.vere.game;

import android.graphics.*;

public abstract class Sprite {
    protected int x, y;//Sprite x, y coordinates
    protected Bitmap bitmap;//Pictures of sprite
    protected boolean visiable = true;//Is the sprite visible
    protected int width, height;//Sprite width and height

    public Sprite(Bitmap bitmap, int x, int y) {
        super();
        this.bitmap = bitmap;
        this.width = bitmap.getWidth();
        this.height = bitmap.getHeight();
        this.x = x;
        this.y = y;
    }

    //if the mouse (x, y) is in area of Sprite
    public boolean contains(int x, int y) {
        if((x - this.x < this.width) && (y - this.y < this.height)){
            return true;
        }
        return false;
    }

    //draw sprite on canvas
    public void draw(Canvas canvas) {
        if (this.isVisiable()) {
            canvas.drawBitmap(this.bitmap, this.x, this.y, null);
        }
    }

    //move sprite on canvas
    //distanceX: The distance moved in the x-axis
    //distanceY: The distance moved in the y-axis
    public void move(int distanceX, int distanceY) {
        this.x += distanceX;
        this.y += distanceY;
    }

    public int getX() {
        return x;
    }
```

```java
public void setX(int x) {
    this.x = x;
}

public int getY() {
    return y;
}

public void setY(int y) {
    this.y = y;
}

public boolean isVisiable() {
    return visiable;
}

public void setVisiable(boolean visiable) {
    this.visiable = visiable;
}

public void setWidth(int width) {
    this.width = width;
}

public int getWidth() {
    return this.width;
}

public void setHeight(int height) {
    this.height = height;
}

public int getHeight() {
    return this.height;
}
}
```

ImageCache.java

```java
package com.vere.game;

import android.graphics.Bitmap;
import java.util.*;

public class ImageCache {
    private static Map<String,Bitmap> cacheMap=new HashMap<String, Bitmap>();

    private ImageCache(){}

    public static void put(String key, Bitmap image){
        cacheMap.put(key, image);
    }

    public static Bitmap get(String key){
        return cacheMap.get(key);
    }
}
```

RedPlane.java

```java
package com.vere.game;

public class RedPlane extends Sprite {

    public RedPlane(int x, int y) {
        super(ImageCache.get("redPlaneBitmap"), x, y);
    }
}
```

BluePlane.java

```java
package com.vere.game;

public class BluePlane extends Sprite {

    public BluePlane(int x, int y) {
        super(ImageCache.get("bluePlaneBitmap"), x, y);
    }
}
```

SpriteFactory.java

```java
package com.vere.game;

public class SpriteFactory {

    public static Sprite create(String type, int x, int y){
        if ("1".equals(type)){
            return new BluePlane(x, y);
        }else if ("2".equals(type)){
            return new RedPlane(x, y);
        }
        return null;
    }

}
```

GameView.java

```java
package com.vere.game;
import android.graphics.Canvas;
import android.graphics.Color;
import android.graphics.Paint;
import android.view.MotionEvent;
import android.view.SurfaceHolder;
import android.view.SurfaceView;

public class GameView extends SurfaceView implements Runnable, SurfaceHolder.Callback {
    private MainActivity gameActivity;
    private boolean isRun = true;
    private SurfaceHolder surfaceHolder;
    private Paint paint;
    private Sprite plane;
    private int canvasWidth, canvasHeight;
    private int downX, downY;//coordinates of the mouse down
    private int moveX, moveY;//coordinates of the mouse move
    private String planeType;

    public GameView(MainActivity gameActivity, String planeType) {
        super(gameActivity);
        this.gameActivity = gameActivity;
        this.planeType = planeType;

        surfaceHolder = this.getHolder();
        surfaceHolder.addCallback(this);
    }
```

```java
public void surfaceCreated(SurfaceHolder holder) {
    this.setFocusable(true);
    this.setFocusableInTouchMode(true);
    this.canvasWidth = this.getWidth(); // get width of canvas
    this.canvasHeight = this.getHeight(); // get height of canvas
    this.surfaceHolder = holder;
    paint = new Paint();

    //create plane SpriteFactory
    plane = SpriteFactory.create(this.planeType, 0, 0);
    plane.setX(this.canvasWidth / 2 - plane.getWidth() / 2);
    plane.setY(this.canvasHeight - plane.getHeight() - 40);

    new Thread(this).start(); // start game loop thread
}

public void surfaceChanged(SurfaceHolder holder, int format, int width, int height) {

}

public void surfaceDestroyed(SurfaceHolder holder) {
    isRun = false;
}

@Override
public boolean onTouchEvent(MotionEvent event) {
    if (event.getAction() == MotionEvent.ACTION_DOWN) {
        downX = (int) event.getX();
        downY = (int) event.getY();
    } else if (event.getAction() == MotionEvent.ACTION_MOVE) {
        moveX = (int) event.getX();
        moveY = (int) event.getY();

        //Calculate the distance moved by the mouse
        int distanceX = moveX - downX;
        int distanceY = moveY - downY;

        if (plane.contains(downX, downY)) {
            //The plane follows the mouse move
            plane.move(distanceX, distanceY);
        }

        //Save moving coordinates to down coordinates
        downX = moveX;
        downY = moveY;
    }
    return true;
}
```

```java
public void drawGame(Canvas canvas) {
    canvas.drawColor(Color.WHITE);
    plane.draw(canvas); //draw plane on canvas
}

// game loop to repeat draw
public void run() {
    while (isRun) {
        Canvas canvas = null;
        try {
            canvas = surfaceHolder.lockCanvas();
            synchronized (surfaceHolder) {
                drawGame(canvas); // draw images of games
            }
            Thread.sleep(50);
        } catch (Exception e) {
            e.printStackTrace();
        } finally {
            if (canvas != null) {
                surfaceHolder.unlockCanvasAndPost(canvas);
            }
        }
    }
}
```

MainActivity.java

```java
package com.vere.game;

import androidx.appcompat.app.AppCompatActivity;
import android.app.AlertDialog;
import android.content.DialogInterface;
import android.graphics.Bitmap;
import android.graphics.BitmapFactory;
import android.os.Bundle;
import android.view.*;
import android.widget.ImageView;
import android.widget.Toast;

public class MainActivity extends AppCompatActivity {
    private AlertDialog dialog;
```

```java
    protected void onCreate(Bundle savedInstanceState) {
        supportRequestWindowFeature(Window.FEATURE_NO_TITLE);
        getWindow().setFlags(WindowManager.LayoutParams.FLAG_FULLSCREEN,
WindowManager.LayoutParams.FLAG_FULLSCREEN);
        super.onCreate(savedInstanceState);

        Bitmap bluePlaneBitmap = BitmapFactory.decodeResource(getResources(), R.drawable.blue_plane);
        ImageCache.put("bluePlaneBitmap", bluePlaneBitmap);
        Bitmap redPlaneBitmap = BitmapFactory.decodeResource(getResources(), R.drawable.red_plane);
        ImageCache.put("redPlaneBitmap", redPlaneBitmap);

        //AlertDialog
        AlertDialog.Builder builder=new AlertDialog.Builder(this);
        //load res->layout->select_plane.xml
        View planeSelectView=View.inflate(this, R.layout.select_plane, null);
        //get ImageView Object
        ImageView btnBluePlane=(ImageView)planeSelectView.findViewById(R.id.bluePlane);
        ImageView btnRedPlane=(ImageView)planeSelectView.findViewById(R.id.redPlane);

        //Set click command event
        btnBluePlane.setOnClickListener(new View.OnClickListener()
        {
            public void onClick(View v)
            {
                MainActivity.this.setContentView(new GameView(MainActivity.this, "1"));
                dialog.dismiss();

            }
        });
        btnRedPlane.setOnClickListener(new View.OnClickListener()
        {
            public void onClick(View v)
            {
                MainActivity.this.setContentView(new GameView(MainActivity.this, "2"));
                dialog.dismiss();

            }
        });

        dialog=builder.create();//build a dialog
        dialog.show();//show dialog

        //replace dialog content view
        dialog.getWindow().setContentView(planeSelectView);
    }
}
```

Iterator Pattern Game

Iterator Pattern : Sequentially access the elements of a collection. Provide a way to access the elements of an aggregate object sequentially without exposing its underlying representation.

1. iterator print bullet list

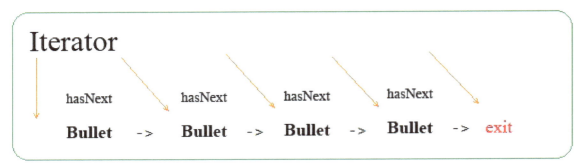

Iterator:

boolean hasNext(): It returns true if Iterator has more element
Object next(): It returns the next element in the list.

1. Create BluePlane on canvas.
2. Create less than100 bullets in Thread run() method. And then load to bulletList
3. Iterator Draw and Move all bullets of bulletList on canvas.

Create less than 100 bullets , the bullets start to move in the top center of plane.

```java
private CopyOnWriteArrayList<Bullet> bulletList = new CopyOnWriteArrayList<~>();
private int bulletSpeed = 8;

public Plane(Bitmap bitmap, int x, int y) {
    super(bitmap, x, y);
}

public void createBullets(){
    if(bulletSpeed == 0) {
        if (this.bulletList.size() < 100) {
            Bullet bullet = new RedBullet( x: -100,  y: -100);
            int x = this.getX() + this.getWidth() / 2 - bullet.getWidth() / 2;
            int y = this.getY() - bullet.getHeight();
            bullet.setX(x);
            bullet.setY(y);
            bullet.setVisible(true);
            this.loadBullet(bullet);
            bulletSpeed = 8;
        }
    }else{
        bulletSpeed --;
    }
}
```

Iterator Draw and Move all bullets on canvas.

```java
public void drawBullets(Canvas canvas) {
    Iterator<Bullet> iter = this.bulletList.iterator();
    while (iter.hasNext()) {
        Bullet bullet = iter.next();
        if (bullet.isVisible()) {
            bullet.draw(canvas);
        }
    }
}

public void moveBullet(int distanceX, int distanceY) {
    Iterator<Bullet> iter = this.bulletList.iterator();
    while (iter.hasNext()) {
        Bullet bullet = iter.next();
        if (bullet.isVisible()) {
            bullet.move(distanceX, distanceY);
        }
    }
}
```

if the bullet move up out of canvas remove it

```java
public void moveBullet(int distanceX, int distanceY) {
    Iterator<Bullet> iter = this.bulletList.iterator();
    while (iter.hasNext()) {
        Bullet bullet = iter.next();
        if (bullet.isVisible()) {
            bullet.move(distanceX, distanceY);
        }
    }

    for (int i = this.bulletList.size() - 1; i >= 0; i--) {
        Bullet bullet = this.bulletList.get(i);
        //if the bullet move up out of canvas remove it
        if (bullet.getY() + bullet.getHeight() <= 0) {
            this.bulletList.remove(bullet);
        }
    }
}
```

Android Emulator - New_Device_1_API_22:5554

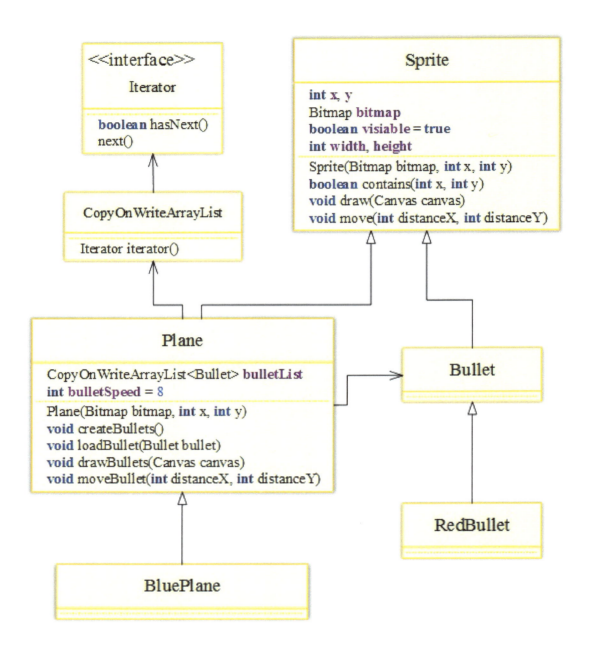

Sprite.java

```java
package com.vere.game;
import android.graphics.*;

public abstract class Sprite {
    protected int x, y;//Sprite x, y coordinates
    protected Bitmap bitmap;//Pictures of sprite
    protected boolean visible = true;//Is the sprite visible
    protected int width, height;//Sprite width and height

    public Sprite(Bitmap bitmap, int x, int y) {
        super();
        this.bitmap = bitmap;
        this.width = bitmap.getWidth();
        this.height = bitmap.getHeight();
        this.x = x;
        this.y = y;
    }

    //if the mouse (x, y) is in area of Sprite
    public boolean contains(int x, int y) {
        if((x - this.x < this.width) && (y - this.y < this.height)){
            return true;
        }
        return false;
    }

    //draw sprite on canvas
    public void draw(Canvas canvas) {
        if (this.isVisible()) {
            canvas.drawBitmap(this.bitmap, this.x, this.y, null);
        }
    }

    public void move(int distanceX, int distanceY) {
        this.x += distanceX;
        this.y += distanceY;
    }

    public int getX() {
        return x;
    }

    public void setX(int x) {
        this.x = x;
    }
```

```java
    public int getY() {
        return y;
    }

    public void setY(int y) {
        this.y = y;
    }

    public boolean isVisible() {
        return visible;
    }

    public void setVisible(boolean visible) {
        this.visible = visible;
    }

    public void setWidth(int width) {
        this.width = width;
    }

    public int getWidth() {
        return this.width;
    }

    public void setHeight(int height) {
        this.height = height;
    }

    public int getHeight() {
        return this.height;
    }
}
```

Bullet.java

```java
package com.vere.game;

import android.graphics.Bitmap;

public class Bullet extends Sprite {

    public Bullet(Bitmap bitmap, int x, int y) {
        super(bitmap, x, y);
    }
}
```

ImageCache.java In the previous chapter flyweight pattern

RedBullet.java in package com.iterator.game;

```java
package com.vere.game;

import android.graphics.Bitmap;

public class RedBullet extends Bullet {

    public RedBullet(int x, int y) {
        super(ImageCache.get("redBulletBitmap"), x, y);
    }
}
```

Plane:

CopyOnWriteArrayList<Bullet> bulletList:. Thread-safe storage of a list of all bullets
void loadBullet(Bullet bullet): Add bullet to bulletList
void drawBullets(Graphics g): Draw all bullets of bulletList on canvas.
void moveBullet(int distanceX, int distanceY): Move all bullets of bulletList on canvas.

Plane.java

```java
package com.vere.game;

import android.graphics.Bitmap;
import android.graphics.Canvas;
import java.util.Iterator;
import java.util.concurrent.CopyOnWriteArrayList;

public class Plane extends Sprite {
    private CopyOnWriteArrayList<Bullet> bulletList = new CopyOnWriteArrayList<Bullet>();
    private int bulletSpeed = 8;

    public Plane(Bitmap bitmap, int x, int y) {
        super(bitmap, x, y);
    }
```

```java
public void createBullets(){
    if(bulletSpeed == 0) {
        if (this.bulletList.size() < 100) {
            Bullet bullet = new RedBullet(-100, -100);
            int x = this.getX() + this.getWidth() / 2 - bullet.getWidth() / 2;
            int y = this.getY() - bullet.getHeight();
            bullet.setX(x);
            bullet.setY(y);
            bullet.setVisible(true);
            this.loadBullet(bullet);
            bulletSpeed = 8;
        }
    }else{
        bulletSpeed --;
    }
}

public void drawBullets(Canvas canvas) {
    Iterator<Bullet> iter = this.bulletList.iterator();
    while (iter.hasNext()) {
        Bullet bullet = iter.next();
        if (bullet.isVisible()) {
            bullet.draw(canvas);
        }
    }
}

public void moveBullet(int distanceX, int distanceY) {
    Iterator<Bullet> iter = this.bulletList.iterator();
    while (iter.hasNext()) {
        Bullet bullet = iter.next();
        if (bullet.isVisible()) {
            bullet.move(distanceX, distanceY);
        }
    }

    for (int i = this.bulletList.size() - 1; i >= 0; i--) {
        Bullet bullet = this.bulletList.get(i);
        //if the bullet move up out of canvas remove it
        if (bullet.getY() + bullet.getHeight() <= 0) {
            this.bulletList.remove(bullet);
        }
    }
}

public void loadBullet(Bullet bullet) {
    bulletList.add(bullet);
}
}
```

BluePlane.java

```java
package com.vere.game;

public class BluePlane extends Plane {

    public BluePlane(int x, int y) {
        super(ImageCache.get("bluePlaneBitmap"), x, y);
    }
}
```

PlaneFactory.java

```java
package com.vere.game;

public class PlaneFactory {

    public static Plane create(String type, int x, int y){
        if ("1".equals(type)){
            return new BluePlane(x, y);
        }else  if ("2".equals(type)){
            return new RedPlane(x, y);
        }
        return null;
    }

}
```

GameView.java

```java
package com.vere.game;
import android.graphics.*;
import android.view.*;

public class GameView extends SurfaceView implements Runnable, SurfaceHolder.Callback {
    private MainActivity gameActivity;
    private boolean isRun = true;
    private SurfaceHolder surfaceHolder;
    private Paint paint;
    private Plane plane;
    private int canvasWidth, canvasHeight;
    private int downX, downY;//coordinates of the mouse down
    private int moveX, moveY;//coordinates of the mouse move
    private String planeType;

    public GameView(MainActivity gameActivity, String planeType) {
        super(gameActivity);
        this.gameActivity = gameActivity;
        this.planeType = planeType;
        surfaceHolder = this.getHolder();
        surfaceHolder.addCallback(this);
    }

    public void surfaceCreated(SurfaceHolder holder) {
        this.setFocusable(true);
        this.setFocusableInTouchMode(true);
        this.canvasWidth = this.getWidth(); // get width of canvas
        this.canvasHeight = this.getHeight(); // get height of canvas
        this.surfaceHolder = holder;
        paint = new Paint();

        //create plane SpriteFactory
        plane = PlaneFactory.create(this.planeType, 0, 0);
        plane.setX(this.canvasWidth / 2 - plane.getWidth() / 2);
        plane.setY(this.canvasHeight - plane.getHeight() - 40);

        new Thread(this).start(); // start game loop thread
    }

    public void surfaceChanged(SurfaceHolder holder, int format, int width, int height) {

    }

    public void surfaceDestroyed(SurfaceHolder holder) {
        isRun = false;
    }
```

```java
public boolean onTouchEvent(MotionEvent event) {
    if (event.getAction() == MotionEvent.ACTION_DOWN) {
        downX = (int) event.getX();
        downY = (int) event.getY();
    } else if (event.getAction() == MotionEvent.ACTION_MOVE) {
        moveX = (int) event.getX();
        moveY = (int) event.getY();

        //Calculate the distance moved by the mouse
        int distanceX = moveX - downX;
        int distanceY = moveY - downY;

        if (plane.contains(downX, downY)) {
            plane.move(distanceX, distanceY);
        }

        downX = moveX;
        downY = moveY;
    }
    return true;
}

public void drawGame(Canvas canvas) {
    canvas.drawColor(Color.WHITE);
    plane.draw(canvas); //draw plane on canvas
    plane.createBullets("2");
    plane.drawBullets(canvas);
    plane.moveBullet(0, -8);
}

public void run() {
    while (isRun) {
        Canvas canvas = null;
        try {
            canvas = surfaceHolder.lockCanvas();
            synchronized (surfaceHolder) {
                drawGame(canvas); // draw images of games
            }
            Thread.sleep(50);
        } catch (Exception e) {
            e.printStackTrace();
        } finally {
            if (canvas != null) {
                surfaceHolder.unlockCanvasAndPost(canvas);
            }
        }
    }
}
}
```

MainActivity.java

```java
package com.vere.game;

import androidx.appcompat.app.AppCompatActivity;

import android.app.AlertDialog;
import android.content.DialogInterface;
import android.graphics.Bitmap;
import android.graphics.BitmapFactory;
import android.os.Bundle;
import android.view.*;
import android.widget.ImageView;
import android.widget.Toast;

public class MainActivity extends AppCompatActivity {

    private AlertDialog dialog;

    @Override
    protected void onCreate(Bundle savedInstanceState) {
        supportRequestWindowFeature(Window.FEATURE_NO_TITLE);
        getWindow().setFlags(WindowManager.LayoutParams.FLAG_FULLSCREEN,
WindowManager.LayoutParams.FLAG_FULLSCREEN);
        super.onCreate(savedInstanceState);

        Bitmap bluePlaneBitmap = BitmapFactory.decodeResource(getResources(), R.drawable.blue_plane);
        ImageCache.put("bluePlaneBitmap", bluePlaneBitmap);
        Bitmap redBulletBitmap = BitmapFactory.decodeResource(getResources(), R.drawable.red_bullet);
        ImageCache.put("redBulletBitmap", redBulletBitmap);

        this.setContentView(new GameView(MainActivity.this, "1"));

    }
}
```

64

Bridge Pattern Game

Bridge Pattern : Separates an object's interface from its implementation. Decouple an abstraction from its implementation so that the two can vary independently.

1. BluePlane can fire BlueBullet.
2. RedPlane can fire RedBullet.
3. BluePlane can fire RedBullet.
4. RedPlane can fire BlueBullet.

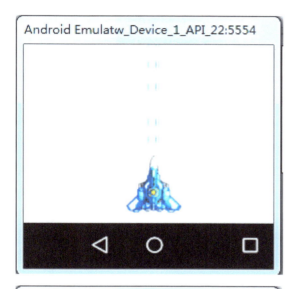
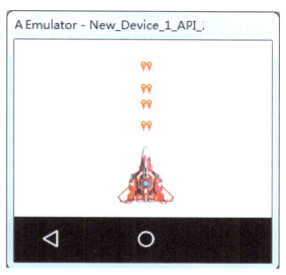

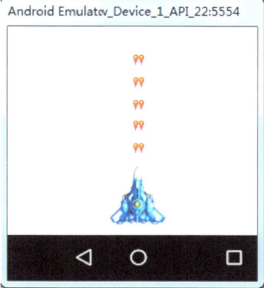
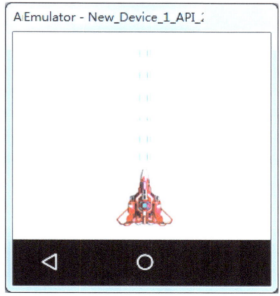

1. BluePlane can fire BlueBullet.

```
plane.createBullets( bulletType: "1");

public void createBullets(String bulletType){
    if(bulletSpeed == 0) {
        if (this.bulletList.size() < 100) {
            Bullet bullet = BulletFactory.create(bulletType,  x: -100,  y: -100);
            int x = this.getX() + this.getWidth() / 2 - bullet.getWidth() / 2;
            int y = this.getY() - bullet.getHeight();
            bullet.setX(x);
            bullet.setY(y);
            bullet.setVisible(true);
            this.loadBullet(bullet);
            bulletSpeed = 8;
        }
    }else{
        bulletSpeed --;
    }
}
```

```
this.setContentView(new GameView(MainActivity.this, "1"));

    //create plane SpriteFactory
    plane = PlaneFactory.create(this.planeType,  x: 0,  y: 0);
    plane.setX(this.canvasWidth / 2 - plane.getWidth() / 2);
    plane.setY(this.canvasHeight - plane.getHeight() - 40);
```

2. BluePlane can fire RedBullet.

```java
plane.createBullets( bulletType: "2");

public void createBullets(String bulletType){
    if(bulletSpeed == 0) {
        if (this.bulletList.size() < 100) {
            Bullet bullet = BulletFactory.create(bulletType,  x: -100,  y: -100);
            int x = this.getX() + this.getWidth() / 2 - bullet.getWidth() / 2;
            int y = this.getY() - bullet.getHeight();
            bullet.setX(x);
            bullet.setY(y);
            bullet.setVisible(true);
            this.loadBullet(bullet);
            bulletSpeed = 8;
        }
    }else{
        bulletSpeed --;
    }
}
```

```java
this.setContentView(new GameView( MainActivity.this, "1"));

//create plane SpriteFactory
plane = PlaneFactory.create(this.planeType,  x: 0,  y: 0);
plane.setX(this.canvasWidth / 2 - plane.getWidth() / 2);
plane.setY(this.canvasHeight - plane.getHeight() - 40);
```

67

UML Diagram

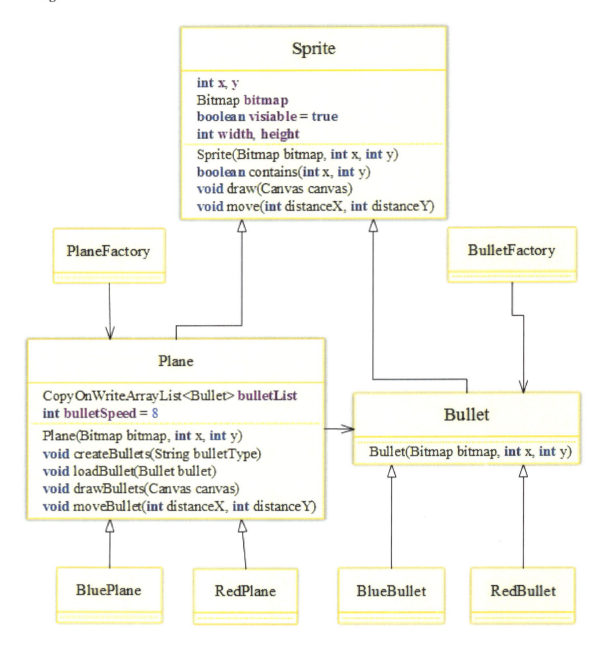

Sprite.java

```java
package com.vere.game;
import android.graphics.*;

public abstract class Sprite {
    protected int x, y;//Sprite x, y coordinates
    protected Bitmap bitmap;//Pictures of sprite
    protected boolean visible = true;//Is the sprite visible
    protected int width, height;//Sprite width and height

    public Sprite(Bitmap bitmap, int x, int y) {
        super();
        this.bitmap = bitmap;
        this.width = bitmap.getWidth();
        this.height = bitmap.getHeight();
        this.x = x;
        this.y = y;
    }

    //if the mouse (x, y) is in area of Sprite
    public boolean contains(int x, int y) {
        if((x - this.x < this.width) && (y - this.y < this.height)){
            return true;
        }
        return false;
    }

    //draw sprite on canvas
    public void draw(Canvas canvas) {
        if (this.isVisible()) {
            canvas.drawBitmap(this.bitmap, this.x, this.y, null);
        }
    }

    public void move(int distanceX, int distanceY) {
        this.x += distanceX;
        this.y += distanceY;
    }

    public int getX() {
        return x;
    }

    public void setX(int x) {
        this.x = x;
    }
```

```java
    public int getY() {
        return y;
    }

    public void setY(int y) {
        this.y = y;
    }

    public boolean isVisible() {
        return visible;
    }

    public void setVisible(boolean visible) {
        this.visible = visible;
    }

    public void setWidth(int width) {
        this.width = width;
    }

    public int getWidth() {
        return this.width;
    }

    public void setHeight(int height) {
        this.height = height;
    }

    public int getHeight() {
        return this.height;
    }
}
```

Bullet.java

```java
package com.vere.game;

import android.graphics.Bitmap;

public class Bullet extends Sprite {

    public Bullet(Bitmap bitmap, int x, int y) {
        super(bitmap, x, y);
    }
}
```

ImageCache.java **In the previous chapter flyweight pattern**

BlueBullet.java

```java
package com.vere.game;

public class BlueBullet extends Bullet {

    public BlueBullet(int x, int y) {
        super(ImageCache.get("blueBulletBitmap"), x, y);
    }
}
```

RedBullet.java

```java
package com.vere.game;

public class RedBullet extends Bullet {

    public RedBullet(int x, int y) {
        super(ImageCache.get("redBulletBitmap"), x, y);
    }
}
```

BulletFactory.java

```java
package com.vere.game;

public class BulletFactory {

    public static Bullet create(String type, int x, int y){
        if ("1".equals(type)){
            return new BlueBullet(x, y);
        }else  if ("2".equals(type)){
            return new RedBullet(x, y);
        }
        return null;
    }

}
```

Plane.java

```java
package com.vere.game;

import android.graphics.*;
import java.util.Iterator;
import java.util.concurrent.CopyOnWriteArrayList;

public class Plane extends Sprite {
    private CopyOnWriteArrayList<Bullet> bulletList = new CopyOnWriteArrayList<Bullet>();
    private int bulletSpeed = 8;

    public Plane(Bitmap bitmap, int x, int y) {
        super(bitmap, x, y);
    }

    public void createBullets(String bulletType){
        if(bulletSpeed == 0) {
            if (this.bulletList.size() < 100) {
                Bullet bullet = BulletFactory.create(bulletType, -100, -100);
                int x = this.getX() + this.getWidth() / 2 - bullet.getWidth() / 2;
                int y = this.getY() - bullet.getHeight();
                bullet.setX(x);
                bullet.setY(y);
                bullet.setVisible(true);
                this.loadBullet(bullet);
                bulletSpeed = 8;
            }
        }else{
            bulletSpeed --;
        }
    }

    public void drawBullets(Canvas canvas) {
        Iterator<Bullet> iter = this.bulletList.iterator();
        while (iter.hasNext()) {
            Bullet bullet = iter.next();
            if (bullet.isVisible()) {
                bullet.draw(canvas);
            }
        }
    }

    public void loadBullet(Bullet bullet) {
        bulletList.add(bullet);
    }
```

```java
    public void moveBullet(int distanceX, int distanceY) {
        Iterator<Bullet> iter = this.bulletList.iterator();
        while (iter.hasNext()) {
            Bullet bullet = iter.next();
            if (bullet.isVisible()) {
                bullet.move(distanceX, distanceY);
            }
        }
        for (int i = this.bulletList.size() - 1; i >= 0; i--) {
            Bullet bullet = this.bulletList.get(i);
            //if the bullet move up out of canvas remove it
            if (bullet.getY() + bullet.getHeight() <= 0) {
                this.bulletList.remove(bullet);
            }
        }
    }
}
```

BluePlane.java

```java
package com.vere.game;
public class BluePlane extends Plane {
    public BluePlane(int x, int y) {
        super(ImageCache.get("bluePlaneBitmap"), x, y);
    }
}
```

RedPlane.java

```java
package com.vere.game;
public class RedPlane extends Plane {
    public RedPlane(int x, int y) {
        super(ImageCache.get("redPlaneBitmap"), x, y);
    }
}
```

PlaneFactory.java

```java
package com.vere.game;
public class PlaneFactory {
    public static Plane create(String type, int x, int y){
        if ("1".equals(type)){
            return new BluePlane(x, y);
        }else  if ("2".equals(type)){
            return new RedPlane(x, y);
        }
        return null;
    }
}
```

GameView.java

```java
package com.vere.game;
import android.graphics.*;
import android.view.*;

public class GameView extends SurfaceView implements Runnable, SurfaceHolder.Callback {
    private MainActivity gameActivity;
    private boolean isRun = true;
    private SurfaceHolder surfaceHolder;
    private Paint paint;
    private Plane plane;
    private int canvasWidth, canvasHeight;
    private int downX, downY;//coordinates of the mouse down
    private int moveX, moveY;//coordinates of the mouse move
    private String planeType;

    public GameView(MainActivity gameActivity, String planeType) {
        super(gameActivity);
        this.gameActivity = gameActivity;
        this.planeType = planeType;
        surfaceHolder = this.getHolder();
        surfaceHolder.addCallback(this);
    }

    public void surfaceCreated(SurfaceHolder holder) {
        this.setFocusable(true);
        this.setFocusableInTouchMode(true);
        this.canvasWidth = this.getWidth(); // get width of canvas
        this.canvasHeight = this.getHeight(); // get height of canvas
        this.surfaceHolder = holder;
        paint = new Paint();

        //create plane SpriteFactory
        plane = PlaneFactory.create(this.planeType, 0, 0);
        plane.setX(this.canvasWidth / 2 - plane.getWidth() / 2);
        plane.setY(this.canvasHeight - plane.getHeight() - 40);

        new Thread(this).start(); // start game loop thread
    }

    public void surfaceChanged(SurfaceHolder holder, int format, int width, int height) {

    }

    public void surfaceDestroyed(SurfaceHolder holder) {
        isRun = false;
    }
```

```java
public boolean onTouchEvent(MotionEvent event) {
    if (event.getAction() == MotionEvent.ACTION_DOWN) {
        downX = (int) event.getX();
        downY = (int) event.getY();
    } else if (event.getAction() == MotionEvent.ACTION_MOVE) {
        moveX = (int) event.getX();
        moveY = (int) event.getY();

        //Calculate the distance moved by the mouse
        int distanceX = moveX - downX;
        int distanceY = moveY - downY;

        if (plane.contains(downX, downY)) {
            plane.move(distanceX, distanceY);
        }

        downX = moveX;
        downY = moveY;
    }
    return true;
}

public void drawGame(Canvas canvas) {
    canvas.drawColor(Color.WHITE);
    plane.draw(canvas); //draw plane on canvas
    plane.createBullets("2");
    plane.drawBullets(canvas);
    plane.moveBullet(0, -8);
}

public void run() {
    while (isRun) {
        Canvas canvas = null;
        try {
            canvas = surfaceHolder.lockCanvas();
            synchronized (surfaceHolder) {
                drawGame(canvas); // draw images of games
            }
            Thread.sleep(50);
        } catch (Exception e) {
            e.printStackTrace();
        } finally {
            if (canvas != null) {
                surfaceHolder.unlockCanvasAndPost(canvas);
            }
        }
    }
}
```

```java
package com.vere.game;

import androidx.appcompat.app.AppCompatActivity;

import android.app.AlertDialog;
import android.content.DialogInterface;
import android.graphics.Bitmap;
import android.graphics.BitmapFactory;
import android.os.Bundle;
import android.view.*;
import android.widget.ImageView;
import android.widget.Toast;

public class MainActivity extends AppCompatActivity {

    @Override
    protected void onCreate(Bundle savedInstanceState) {
        supportRequestWindowFeature(Window.FEATURE_NO_TITLE);
        getWindow().setFlags(WindowManager.LayoutParams.FLAG_FULLSCREEN,
WindowManager.LayoutParams.FLAG_FULLSCREEN);
        super.onCreate(savedInstanceState);

        Bitmap bluePlaneBitmap = BitmapFactory.decodeResource(getResources(), R.drawable.blue_plane);
        ImageCache.put("bluePlaneBitmap", bluePlaneBitmap);
        Bitmap redPlaneBitmap = BitmapFactory.decodeResource(getResources(), R.drawable.red_plane);
        ImageCache.put("redPlaneBitmap", redPlaneBitmap);
        Bitmap redBulletBitmap = BitmapFactory.decodeResource(getResources(), R.drawable.red_bullet);
        ImageCache.put("redBulletBitmap", redBulletBitmap);
        Bitmap blueBulletBitmap = BitmapFactory.decodeResource(getResources(), R.drawable.blue_bullet);
        ImageCache.put("blueBulletBitmap", blueBulletBitmap);
        Bitmap missileBulletBitmap = BitmapFactory.decodeResource(getResources(),
R.drawable.missile_bullet);
        ImageCache.put("missileBulletBitmap", missileBulletBitmap);

        this.setContentView(new GameView(MainActivity.this, "1"));
    }
}
```

Chain Pattern Game

Chain Pattern : A way of passing a request between a chain of objects. Avoid coupling the sender of a request to its receiver by giving more than one object a chance to handle the request. Chain the receiving objects and pass the request along the chain until an object handles it.

1. Enemy plane appear from the top of the screen every once in a while

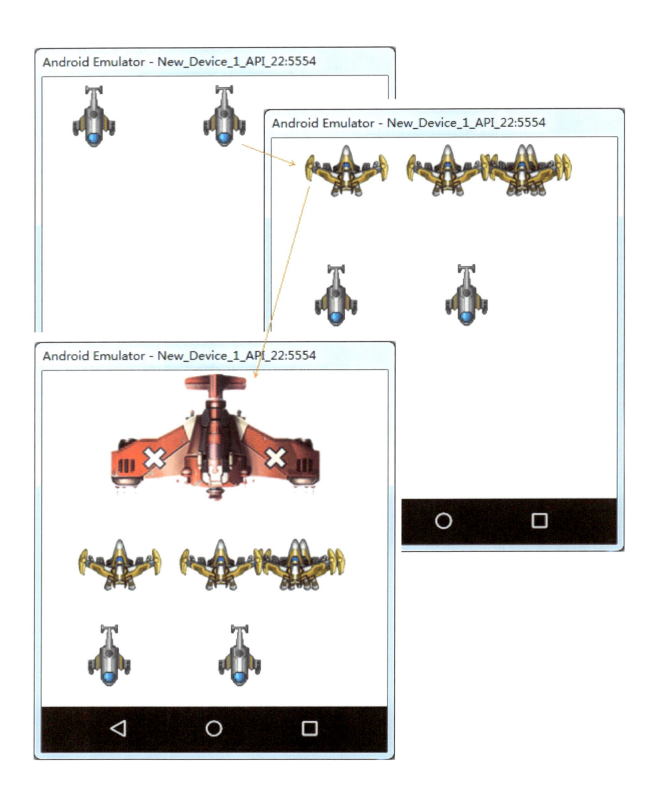

1. 2 enemy planes appear in 80 seconds

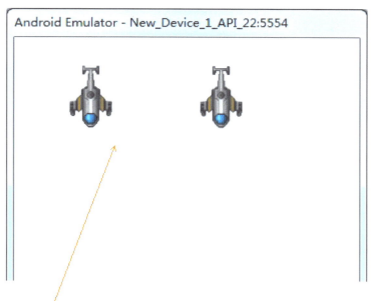

```java
@Override
public List<Sprite> create() {
    Random rn = new Random();
    List<Sprite> spriteList = new ArrayList<~>();
    for (int i = 0; i < 2; i++) {
        int x = rn.nextInt( bound: canvasWidth - enemyPlaneImage.getWidth());
        int y = -enemyPlaneImage.getHeight();
        Sprite enemyPlane = new EnemyPlane(enemyPlaneImage, x, y);
        spriteList.add(enemyPlane);
    }
    return spriteList;
}
```

2. 4 enemy planes appear after 80 seconds

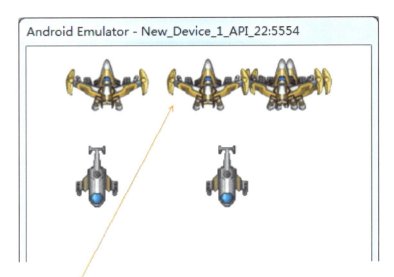

```java
@Override
public List<Sprite> create() {
    Random rn = new Random();
    List<Sprite> spriteList = new ArrayList<~>();
    for (int i = 0; i < 4; i++) {
        int x = rn.nextInt( bound: canvasWidth - enemyPlaneImage.getWidth());
        int y = -enemyPlaneImage.getHeight();
        Sprite enemyPlane = new EnemyPlane(enemyPlaneImage, x, y);
        spriteList.add(enemyPlane);
    }
    return spriteList;
}
```

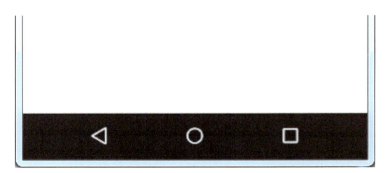

3. boss enemy planes appear after 80 seconds

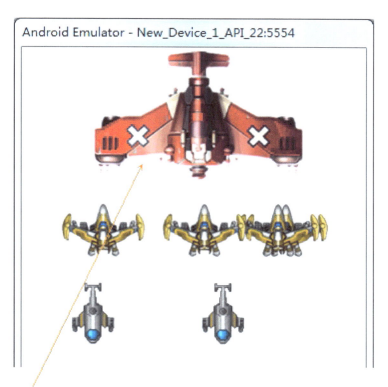

```java
@Override
public List<Sprite> create() {
    Random rn = new Random();
    List<Sprite> spriteList = new ArrayList<~>();
    int x = rn.nextInt( bound: canvasWidth - enemyPlaneImage.getWidth());
    int y = -enemyPlaneImage.getHeight();
    Sprite enemyPlane = new EnemyPlane(enemyPlaneImage, x, y);
    spriteList.add(enemyPlane);
    return spriteList;
}
```

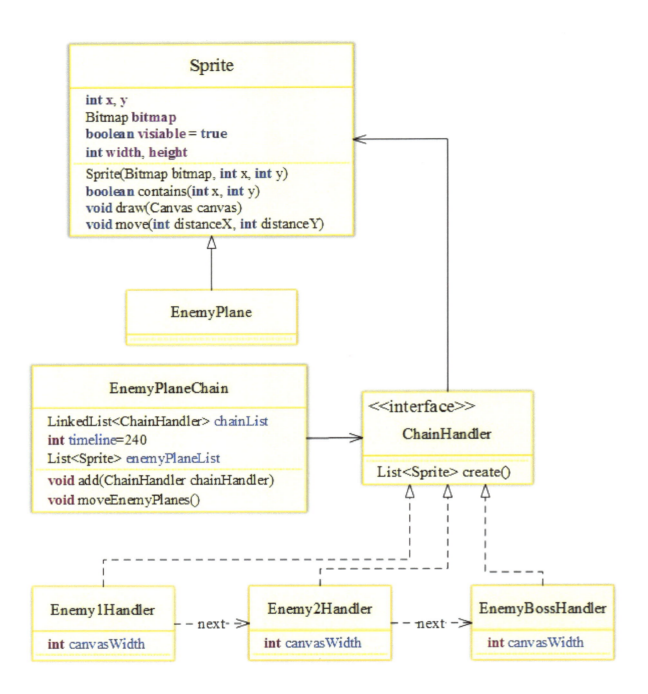

Sprite.java

```java
package com.vere.game;

import android.graphics.*;

public abstract class Sprite {
    protected int x, y;//Sprite x, y coordinates
    protected Bitmap bitmap;//Pictures of sprite
    protected boolean visible = true;//Is the sprite visible
    protected int width, height;//Sprite width and height

    public Sprite(Bitmap bitmap, int x, int y) {
        super();
        this.bitmap = bitmap;
        this.width = bitmap.getWidth();
        this.height = bitmap.getHeight();
        this.x = x;
        this.y = y;
    }

    //if the mouse (x, y) is in area of Sprite
    public boolean contains(int x, int y) {
        if((x - this.x < this.width) && (y - this.y < this.height)){
            return true;
        }
        return false;
    }

    //draw sprite on canvas
    public void draw(Canvas canvas) {
        if (this.isVisible()) {
            canvas.drawBitmap(this.bitmap, this.x, this.y, null);
        }
    }

    //move sprite on canvas
    //distanceX: The distance moved in the x-axis
    //distanceY: The distance moved in the y-axis
    public void move(int distanceX, int distanceY) {
        this.x += distanceX;
        this.y += distanceY;
    }

    public int getX() {
        return x;
    }
```

```java
    public void setX(int x) {
        this.x = x;
    }

    public int getY() {
        return y;
    }

    public void setY(int y) {
        this.y = y;
    }

    public boolean isVisible() {
        return visible;
    }

    public void setVisible(boolean visible) {
        this.visible = visible;
    }

    public void setWidth(int width) {
        this.width = width;
    }

    public int getWidth() {
        return this.width;
    }

    public void setHeight(int height) {
        this.height = height;
    }

    public int getHeight() {
        return this.height;
    }

    public Bitmap getBitmap() {
        return bitmap;
    }

    public void setBitmap(Bitmap bitmap) {
        this.bitmap = bitmap;
    }
}
```

EnemyPlane.java

```java
package com.vere.game;

import android.graphics.Bitmap;

public class EnemyPlane extends Sprite {

    public EnemyPlane(Bitmap bitmap, int x, int y) {
        super(bitmap, x, y);
    }
}
```

ChainHandler.java

```java
package com.vere.game;

import java.util.List;

public interface ChainHandler {

    public List<Sprite> create();
}
```

ImageCache.java In the previous chapter flyweight pattern

Enemy1Handler:

List<Sprite> create(): Create 2 enemy planes randomly appearing from the top of the screen

Enemy1Handler.java

```java
package com.vere.game;

import android.graphics.Bitmap;

import java.util.*;

public class Enemy1Handler implements ChainHandler {

    private Bitmap enemyPlaneImage;
    private int canvasWidth;

    public Enemy1Handler(int canvasWidth) {
        this.enemyPlaneImage = ImageCache.get("enemyPlane1Bitmap");
        this.canvasWidth = canvasWidth;
    }

    @Override
    public List<Sprite> create() {
        Random rn = new Random();
        List<Sprite> spriteList = new ArrayList<Sprite>();
        for (int i = 0; i < 2; i++) {
            int x = rn.nextInt(canvasWidth - enemyPlaneImage.getWidth());
            int y = -enemyPlaneImage.getHeight();
            Sprite enemyPlane = new EnemyPlane(enemyPlaneImage, x, y);
            spriteList.add(enemyPlane);
        }
        return spriteList;
    }

}
```

Enemy2Handler:

List<Sprite> create(): Create 4 enemy planes randomly appearing from the top of the screen

Enemy2Handler.java

```java
package com.vere.game;

import android.graphics.Bitmap;

import java.util.ArrayList;
import java.util.List;
import java.util.Random;

public class Enemy2Handler implements ChainHandler {

    private Bitmap enemyPlaneImage;
    private int canvasWidth;

    public Enemy2Handler(int canvasWidth) {
        this.enemyPlaneImage = ImageCache.get("enemyPlane2Bitmap");
        this.canvasWidth = canvasWidth;
    }

    @Override
    public List<Sprite> create() {
        Random rn = new Random();
        List<Sprite> spriteList = new ArrayList<Sprite>();
        for (int i = 0; i < 4; i++) {
            int x = rn.nextInt(canvasWidth - enemyPlaneImage.getWidth());
            int y = -enemyPlaneImage.getHeight();
            Sprite enemyPlane = new EnemyPlane(enemyPlaneImage, x, y);
            spriteList.add(enemyPlane);
        }
        return spriteList;
    }

}
```

EnemyBossHandler:

List<Sprite> create(): Create boss enemy planes randomly appearing from the top of the screen

EnemyBossHandler.java

```java
package com.vere.game;

import android.graphics.Bitmap;

import java.util.ArrayList;
import java.util.List;
import java.util.Random;

public class EnemyBossHandler implements ChainHandler {

    private Bitmap enemyPlaneImage;
    private int canvasWidth;

    public EnemyBossHandler(int canvasWidth) {
        this.enemyPlaneImage = ImageCache.get("enemyBossBitmap");
        this.canvasWidth = canvasWidth;
    }

    @Override
    public List<Sprite> create() {
        Random rn = new Random();
        List<Sprite> spriteList = new ArrayList<Sprite>();
        int x = rn.nextInt(canvasWidth - enemyPlaneImage.getWidth());
        int y = -enemyPlaneImage.getHeight();
        Sprite enemyPlane = new EnemyPlane(enemyPlaneImage, x, y);
        spriteList.add(enemyPlane);
        return spriteList;
    }

}
```

EnemyPlaneChain:

LinkedList<ChainHandler> chainList: all enemy plane in the chainList
void add(ChainHandler chainHandler): add enemy plane to chainList
int timeline=240: enemy plane show every 240/80=3 second.
void moveEnemyPlanes(): move enemy plane

EnemyPlaneChain.java

```java
package com.vere.game;


import android.graphics.Canvas;

import java.util.*;

public class EnemyPlaneChain {
    private LinkedList<ChainHandler> chainList =new LinkedList<ChainHandler>();
    private int timeline=240;
    private List<Sprite> enemyPlaneList = new ArrayList<Sprite>();

    public void add(ChainHandler chainHandler){
        chainList.add(chainHandler);
    }

    public void moveEnemyPlanes(Canvas canvas){
        if(enemyPlaneList == null){
            return;
        }

        if(timeline >0 && timeline % 80 == 0 && chainList.size() >0){
            ChainHandler currentChainHandler = chainList.poll();
            List<Sprite> spriteList= currentChainHandler.create();
            enemyPlaneList.addAll(spriteList);
        }

        for(int i=0;i<enemyPlaneList.size();i++){
            Sprite enemyPlane = enemyPlaneList.get(i);
            enemyPlane.draw(canvas);
            enemyPlane.move(0, 5);
        }

        timeline -- ;
    }
}
```

GameView.java

```java
package com.vere.game;

import android.graphics.*;
import android.view.*;

public class GameView extends SurfaceView implements Runnable, SurfaceHolder.Callback {
    private MainActivity gameActivity;
    private boolean isRun = true;
    private SurfaceHolder surfaceHolder;
    private Paint paint;
    private int canvasWidth, canvasHeight;
    private String planeType;
    private EnemyPlaneChain enemyPlaneChain;

    public GameView(MainActivity gameActivity,String planeType) {
        super(gameActivity);
        this.gameActivity = gameActivity;
        this.planeType = planeType;

        surfaceHolder = this.getHolder();
        surfaceHolder.addCallback(this);
    }

    public void surfaceCreated(SurfaceHolder holder) {
        this.setFocusable(true);
        this.setFocusableInTouchMode(true);
        this.canvasWidth = this.getWidth(); // get width of canvas
        this.canvasHeight = this.getHeight(); // get height of canvas
        this.surfaceHolder = holder;
        paint = new Paint();

        enemyPlaneChain = new EnemyPlaneChain();
        enemyPlaneChain.add(new Enemy1Handler(this.canvasWidth));
        enemyPlaneChain.add(new Enemy2Handler(this.canvasWidth));
        enemyPlaneChain.add(new EnemyBossHandler(this.canvasWidth));

        new Thread(this).start(); // start game loop thread
    }

    public void surfaceChanged(SurfaceHolder holder, int format, int width, int height) {

    }

    public void surfaceDestroyed(SurfaceHolder holder) {
        isRun = false;
    }
```

```java
public void drawGame(Canvas canvas) {
    canvas.drawColor(Color.WHITE);
    enemyPlaneChain.moveEnemyPlanes(canvas);
}

// game loop to repeat draw
public void run() {
    while (isRun) {
        Canvas canvas = null;
        try {
            canvas = surfaceHolder.lockCanvas();
            synchronized (surfaceHolder) {
                drawGame(canvas); // draw images of games
            }
            Thread.sleep(50);
        } catch (Exception e) {
            e.printStackTrace();
        } finally {
            if (canvas != null) {
                surfaceHolder.unlockCanvasAndPost(canvas);
            }
        }
    }
}
```

MainActivity.java

```java
package com.vere.game;

import androidx.appcompat.app.AppCompatActivity;

import android.app.AlertDialog;
import android.content.DialogInterface;
import android.graphics.Bitmap;
import android.graphics.BitmapFactory;
import android.os.Bundle;
import android.view.*;
import android.widget.ImageView;
import android.widget.Toast;

public class MainActivity extends AppCompatActivity {

    @Override
    protected void onCreate(Bundle savedInstanceState) {
        supportRequestWindowFeature(Window.FEATURE_NO_TITLE);
        getWindow().setFlags(WindowManager.LayoutParams.FLAG_FULLSCREEN,
WindowManager.LayoutParams.FLAG_FULLSCREEN);
        super.onCreate(savedInstanceState);

        Bitmap bluePlaneBitmap = BitmapFactory.decodeResource(getResources(), R.drawable.blue_plane);
        ImageCache.put("bluePlaneBitmap", bluePlaneBitmap);
        Bitmap redPlaneBitmap = BitmapFactory.decodeResource(getResources(), R.drawable.red_plane);
        ImageCache.put("redPlaneBitmap", redPlaneBitmap);
        Bitmap redBulletBitmap = BitmapFactory.decodeResource(getResources(), R.drawable.red_bullet);
        ImageCache.put("redBulletBitmap", redBulletBitmap);
        Bitmap blueBulletBitmap = BitmapFactory.decodeResource(getResources(), R.drawable.blue_bullet);
        ImageCache.put("blueBulletBitmap", blueBulletBitmap);
        Bitmap enemyPlane1Bitmap = BitmapFactory.decodeResource(getResources(),
R.drawable.enemy_plane);
        ImageCache.put("enemyPlane1Bitmap", enemyPlane1Bitmap);
        Bitmap enemyPlane2Bitmap = BitmapFactory.decodeResource(getResources(),
R.drawable.enemy_plane2);
        ImageCache.put("enemyPlane2Bitmap", enemyPlane2Bitmap);
        Bitmap enemyBossBitmap = BitmapFactory.decodeResource(getResources(), R.drawable.boss);
        ImageCache.put("enemyBossBitmap", enemyBossBitmap);

        this.setContentView(new GameView(MainActivity.this, "1"));

    }
}
```

Observer Pattern Game

1. BluePlane collision with EnemyPlane notify reduced life by 1
2. Bullet collision with EnemyPlane notify score plus 100

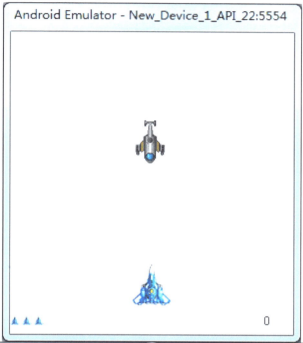

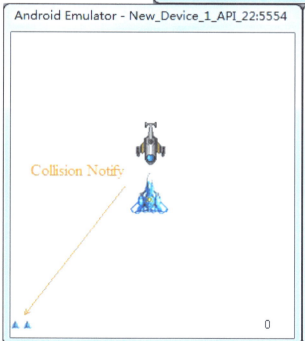

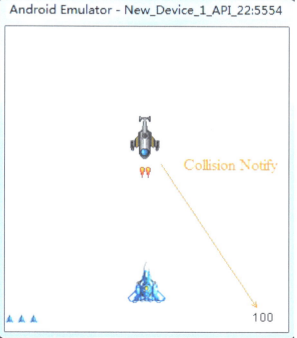

Bullet collision with EnemyPlane notify score plus 100

```java
for (int i = 0; i < enemyPlaneList.size(); i++) {
    Sprite enemyPlane = enemyPlaneList.get(i);
    for(int j=0; j<bulletList.size();j++) {
        Bullet bullet = bulletList.get(j);
        if (bullet.collideWith(enemyPlane)) {
            enemyPlane.setVisible(false);
            bullet.setVisible(false);

            ObserverData data = new ObserverData();
            data.setNotifyType(NotifyType.INCREMENT_SCORE);
            data.setScore(100);
            plane.notifyAll(data);
        }
```

Android Emulator

Collision Notify

100

```java
public void draw(Canvas canvas, Paint paint){
    paint.setColor(Color.RED);
    paint.setTextSize(40);
    canvas.drawText(String.valueOf(score), x, y, paint);
}
public void update(ObserverData data) {
    if(data.getNotifyType() == NotifyType.INCREMENT_SCORE){
        this.score +=data.getScore();
    }
}
```

BluePlane collision with EnemyPlane notify reduced life by 1

```
if (plane.collideWith(enemyPlane)) {
    enemyPlane.setVisible(false);

    ObserverData data = new ObserverData();
    data.setNotifyType(NotifyType.PLANE_DESTROTRY);
    plane.notifyAll(data);
```

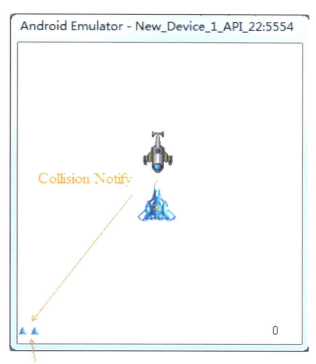

```
public void draw(Canvas canvas){
    for(int i =0;i<lifeCount;i++){
        canvas.drawBitmap(this.bitmap,i*(this.width+2),this.canvasHeight-80, null);
    }
}
public void update(ObserverData data) {
    if(data.getNotifyType() == NotifyType.PLANE_DESTROTRY){
        this.lifeCount --;
    }
}
```

Observer:

void update(ObserverData data): Shoot down an enemy plane to notify to increase score points by 100. Our plane collided with an enemy plane to destroy a life.

Plane:

void registerObserver(Observer observer): register PlaneLife and PlaneScore as observer.
void notifyAll(ObserverData data): notify all observer to update ObserverData

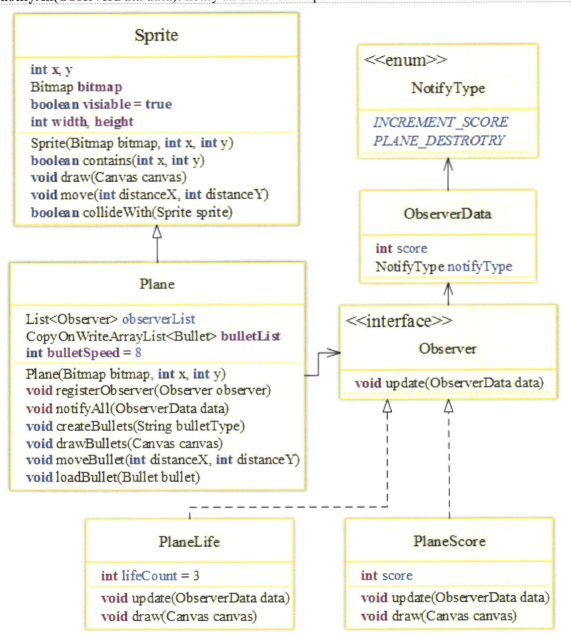

```java
public enum NotifyType {
    INCREMENT_SCORE,
    PLANE_DESTROTRY
}
```

ObserverData.java

```java
public class ObserverData {
    private int score;
    private NotifyType notifyType;

    public int getScore() {
        return score;
    }
    public void setScore(int score) {
        this.score = score;
    }
    public NotifyType getNotifyType() {
        return notifyType;
    }
    public void setNotifyType(NotifyType notifyType) {
        this.notifyType = notifyType;
    }
}
```

Observer:

void update(ObserverData data): Shoot down an enemy plane to notify to increase score points by 100. Our plane collided with an enemy plane to destroy a life.

Observer.java

```java
public interface Observer {

    public void update(ObserverData data);
}
```

ImageCache.java In the previous chapter

PlaneLife.java

```java
package com.vere.game;

import android.graphics.Canvas;

public class PlaneLife  extends Sprite implements Observer{
    protected int lifeCount = 3;
    private int canvasWidth;
    private int canvasHeight;

    public PlaneLife(int x, int y,int canvasWidth, int canvasHeight) {
        super(ImageCache.get("bluePlaneLifeBitmap"), x, y);
        this.canvasWidth = canvasWidth;
        this.canvasHeight = canvasHeight;
    }

    public void draw(Canvas canvas){
        for(int i =0;i<lifeCount;i++){
            canvas.drawBitmap(this.bitmap, i*(this.width+2), this.canvasHeight-80,null);
        }
    }

    @Override
    public void update(ObserverData data) {
        if(data.getNotifyType() == NotifyType.PLANE_DESTROTRY){
            this.lifeCount --;
        }
    }
}
```

PlaneScore.java

```java
package com.vere.game;

import android.graphics.Canvas;
import android.graphics.Color;
import android.graphics.Paint;

public class PlaneScore  implements Observer{
    protected int x; // x coordinate of Canvas
    protected int y; // y coordinate of Canvas
    protected int score;
    private int canvasWidth;
    private int canvasHeight;

    public PlaneScore(int x, int y,int canvasWidth, int canvasHeight) {
        this.canvasWidth = canvasWidth;
        this.canvasHeight = canvasHeight;
        this.x = canvasWidth-100;
        this.y= canvasHeight-30;
    }

    public void draw(Canvas canvas, Paint paint){
        paint.setColor(Color.RED);
        paint.setTextSize(40);
        canvas.drawText(String.valueOf(score), x, y, paint);
    }

    public void update(ObserverData data) {
        if(data.getNotifyType() == NotifyType.INCREMENT_SCORE){
            this.score +=data.getScore();
        }
    }

    public void setX(int x) {
        this.x = x;
    }

    public void setY(int y) {
        this.y = y;
    }
}
```

Sprite.java

```java
package com.vere.game;
import android.graphics.*;
public abstract class Sprite {
    protected int x, y;//Sprite x, y coordinates
    protected Bitmap bitmap;//Pictures of sprite
    protected boolean visible = true;//Is the sprite visible
    protected int width, height;//Sprite width and height
    public Sprite(Bitmap bitmap, int x, int y) {
        super();
        this.bitmap = bitmap;
        this.width = bitmap.getWidth();
        this.height = bitmap.getHeight();
        this.x = x;
        this.y = y;
    }

    public boolean contains(int x, int y) {
        if((x - this.x < this.width) && (y - this.y < this.height)){
            return true;
        }
        return false;
    }

    public void draw(Canvas canvas) {
        if (this.isVisible()) {
            canvas.drawBitmap(this.bitmap, this.x, this.y, null);
        }
    }

    public void move(int distanceX, int distanceY) {
        this.x += distanceX;
        this.y += distanceY;
    }

    public boolean collideWith(Sprite sprite){
        if(this.isVisible() && sprite.isVisible()){
            int centerX = this.x + this.getWidth()/2;
            int centerY = this.y + this.getHeight()/2;
            int spriteCenterX = sprite.getX() + sprite.getWidth()/2;
            int spriteCenterY = sprite.getY() + sprite.getHeight()/2;
            if(Math.abs(centerX - spriteCenterX) < (this.width/2 + sprite.getWidth()/2)
                    &&
                    Math.abs(centerY - spriteCenterY) < (this.height/2 + sprite.getHeight()/2))
                return true;
            else
                return false;
        }
        return false;
    }
```

```java
   public int getX() {
      return x;
   }

   public void setX(int x) {
      this.x = x;
   }

   public int getY() {
      return y;
   }

   public void setY(int y) {
      this.y = y;
   }

   public boolean isVisible() {
      return visible;
   }

   public void setVisible(boolean visible) {
      this.visible = visible;
   }

   public void setWidth(int width) {
      this.width = width;
   }
   public int getWidth() {
      return this.width;
   }


   public void setHeight(int height) {
      this.height = height;
   }

   public int getHeight() {
      return this.height;
   }

   public Bitmap getBitmap() {
      return bitmap;
   }

   public void setBitmap(Bitmap bitmap) {
      this.bitmap = bitmap;
   }
}
```

Plane.java

```java
package com.vere.game;

import android.graphics.Bitmap;
import android.graphics.Canvas;

import java.util.ArrayList;
import java.util.Iterator;
import java.util.List;
import java.util.concurrent.CopyOnWriteArrayList;

public class Plane extends Sprite {
    private CopyOnWriteArrayList<Bullet> bulletList = new CopyOnWriteArrayList<Bullet>();
    private int bulletSpeed = 8;
    protected List<Observer> observerList=new ArrayList<Observer>();

    public Plane(Bitmap bitmap, int x, int y) {
        super(bitmap, x, y);
    }

    public void createBullets(String bulletType){
        if(bulletSpeed == 0) {
            if (this.bulletList.size() < 100) {
                Bullet bullet = BulletFactory.create(bulletType, -100, -100);
                int x = this.getX() + this.getWidth() / 2 - bullet.getWidth() / 2;
                int y = this.getY() - bullet.getHeight();
                bullet.setX(x);
                bullet.setY(y);
                bullet.setVisible(true);
                this.loadBullet(bullet);
                bulletSpeed = 8;
            }
        }else{
            bulletSpeed --;
        }
    }

    public void drawBullets(Canvas canvas) {
        Iterator<Bullet> iter = this.bulletList.iterator();
        while (iter.hasNext()) {
            Bullet bullet = iter.next();
            if (bullet.isVisible()) {
                bullet.draw(canvas);
            }
        }
    }
```

```java
public void moveBullet(int distanceX, int distanceY) {
    Iterator<Bullet> iter = this.bulletList.iterator();
    while (iter.hasNext()) {
        Bullet bullet = iter.next();
        if (bullet.isVisible()) {
            bullet.move(distanceX, distanceY);
        }
    }

    for (int i = this.bulletList.size() - 1; i >= 0; i--) {
        Bullet bullet = this.bulletList.get(i);
        //if the bullet move up out of canvas remove it
        if (bullet.getY() + bullet.getHeight() <= 0) {
            this.bulletList.remove(bullet);
        }
    }
}

public void loadBullet(Bullet bullet) {
    bulletList.add(bullet);
}

public void registerObserver(Observer observer){
    observerList.add(observer);
}

public void notifyAll(ObserverData data){
    for(int i=0;i<observerList.size();i++){
        Observer observer=observerList.get(i);
        observer.update(data);
    }
}

public CopyOnWriteArrayList<Bullet> getBulletList() {
    return bulletList;
}
}
```

Copy all previous chapter chain pattern code here

GameView.java

```java
package com.vere.game;

import android.graphics.*;
import android.view.*;
import java.util.List;
import java.util.concurrent.CopyOnWriteArrayList;

public class GameView extends SurfaceView implements Runnable, SurfaceHolder.Callback {
    private MainActivity gameActivity;
    private boolean isRun = true;
    private SurfaceHolder surfaceHolder;
    private Paint paint;
    private Plane plane;
    private int canvasWidth, canvasHeight;
    private int downX, downY;//coordinates of the mouse down
    private int moveX, moveY;//coordinates of the mouse move
    private String planeType;
    private EnemyPlaneChain enemyPlaneChain;
    private PlaneLife planeLife;
    private PlaneScore planeScore;

    public GameView(MainActivity gameActivity, String planeType) {
        super(gameActivity);
        this.gameActivity = gameActivity;
        this.planeType = planeType;

        surfaceHolder = this.getHolder();
        surfaceHolder.addCallback(this);
    }

    public void surfaceCreated(SurfaceHolder holder) {
        this.setFocusable(true);
        this.setFocusableInTouchMode(true);
        this.canvasWidth = this.getWidth(); // get width of canvas
        this.canvasHeight = this.getHeight(); // get height of canvas
        this.surfaceHolder = holder;
        paint = new Paint();

        //create plane SpriteFactory
        plane = PlaneFactory.create(this.planeType, 0, 0);
        plane.setX(this.canvasWidth / 2 - plane.getWidth() / 2);
        plane.setY(this.canvasHeight - plane.getHeight() - 40);
```

```java
        enemyPlaneChain = new EnemyPlaneChain();
        enemyPlaneChain.add(new Enemy1Handler(canvasWidth));
        enemyPlaneChain.add(new Enemy2Handler(canvasWidth));
        enemyPlaneChain.add(new EnemyBossHandler(canvasWidth));

        planeLife =  new PlaneLife(0, 0, canvasWidth, canvasHeight);
        plane.registerObserver(planeLife);

        planeScore=new PlaneScore(0,0,canvasWidth,canvasHeight );
        plane.registerObserver(planeScore);

        new Thread(this).start(); // start game loop thread
    }

    public void surfaceChanged(SurfaceHolder holder, int format, int width, int height) {

    }

    public void surfaceDestroyed(SurfaceHolder holder) {
        isRun = false;
    }

    @Override
    public boolean onTouchEvent(MotionEvent event) {
        if (event.getAction() == MotionEvent.ACTION_DOWN) {
            downX = (int) event.getX();
            downY = (int) event.getY();
        } else if (event.getAction() == MotionEvent.ACTION_MOVE) {
            moveX = (int) event.getX();
            moveY = (int) event.getY();

            //Calculate the distance moved by the mouse
            int distanceX = moveX - downX;
            int distanceY = moveY - downY;

            if (plane.contains(downX, downY)) {
                //The plane follows the mouse move
                plane.move(distanceX, distanceY);
            }

            //Save moving coordinates to down coordinates
            downX = moveX;
            downY = moveY;
        }
        return true;
    }
```

```java
public void drawGame(Canvas canvas) {
    canvas.drawColor(Color.WHITE);
    plane.draw(canvas); //draw plane on canvas

    plane.createBullets("2");
    plane.drawBullets(canvas);
    plane.moveBullet(0, -8);

    planeLife.draw(canvas);
    planeScore.draw(canvas, paint);

    enemyPlaneChain.moveEnemyPlanes(canvas);

    collideCheck();
}

private void collideCheck() {
    List<Sprite> enemyPlaneList = enemyPlaneChain.getEnemyPlaneList();
    CopyOnWriteArrayList<Bullet> bulletList = plane.getBulletList();
    for (int i = 0; i < enemyPlaneList.size(); i++) {
        Sprite enemyPlane = enemyPlaneList.get(i);
        for(int j=0; j<bulletList.size();j++) {
            Bullet bullet = bulletList.get(j);
            if (bullet.collideWith(enemyPlane)) {
                enemyPlane.setVisible(false);
                bullet.setVisible(false);

                ObserverData data = new ObserverData();
                data.setNotifyType(NotifyType.INCREMENT_SCORE);
                data.setScore(100);
                plane.notifyAll(data);
            }

            if (plane.collideWith(enemyPlane)) {
                enemyPlane.setVisible(false);

                ObserverData data = new ObserverData();
                data.setNotifyType(NotifyType.PLANE_DESTROTRY);
                plane.notifyAll(data);

                plane.setX(this.canvasWidth / 2 - plane.getWidth() / 2);
                plane.setY(this.canvasHeight - plane.getHeight() - 30);
            }
        }
    }
}
```

```java
// game loop to repeat draw
public void run() {
    while (isRun) {
        Canvas canvas = null;
        try {
            canvas = surfaceHolder.lockCanvas();
            synchronized (surfaceHolder) {
                drawGame(canvas); // draw images of games
            }
            Thread.sleep(50);
        } catch (Exception e) {
            e.printStackTrace();
        } finally {
            if (canvas != null) {
                surfaceHolder.unlockCanvasAndPost(canvas);
            }
        }
    }
}
```

MainActivity.java

```java
package com.vere.game;

import androidx.appcompat.app.AppCompatActivity;

import android.app.AlertDialog;
import android.content.DialogInterface;
import android.graphics.Bitmap;
import android.graphics.BitmapFactory;
import android.os.Bundle;
import android.view.*;
import android.widget.ImageView;
import android.widget.Toast;

public class MainActivity extends AppCompatActivity {

    @Override
    protected void onCreate(Bundle savedInstanceState) {
        supportRequestWindowFeature(Window.FEATURE_NO_TITLE);
        getWindow().setFlags(WindowManager.LayoutParams.FLAG_FULLSCREEN,
WindowManager.LayoutParams.FLAG_FULLSCREEN);
        super.onCreate(savedInstanceState);
```

```java
        Bitmap bluePlaneBitmap = BitmapFactory.decodeResource(getResources(), R.drawable.blue_plane);
        ImageCache.put("bluePlaneBitmap", bluePlaneBitmap);
        Bitmap redPlaneBitmap = BitmapFactory.decodeResource(getResources(), R.drawable.red_plane);
        ImageCache.put("redPlaneBitmap", redPlaneBitmap);
        Bitmap redBulletBitmap = BitmapFactory.decodeResource(getResources(), R.drawable.red_bullet);
        ImageCache.put("redBulletBitmap", redBulletBitmap);
        Bitmap blueBulletBitmap = BitmapFactory.decodeResource(getResources(), R.drawable.blue_bullet);
        ImageCache.put("blueBulletBitmap", blueBulletBitmap);
        Bitmap enemyPlane1Bitmap = BitmapFactory.decodeResource(getResources(),
R.drawable.enemy_plane);
        ImageCache.put("enemyPlane1Bitmap", enemyPlane1Bitmap);
        Bitmap enemyPlane2Bitmap = BitmapFactory.decodeResource(getResources(),
R.drawable.enemy_plane2);
        ImageCache.put("enemyPlane2Bitmap", enemyPlane2Bitmap);
        Bitmap enemyBossBitmap = BitmapFactory.decodeResource(getResources(), R.drawable.boss);
        ImageCache.put("enemyBossBitmap", enemyBossBitmap);
        Bitmap bluePlaneLifeBitmap = BitmapFactory.decodeResource(getResources(),
R.drawable.blue_plane_small);
        ImageCache.put("bluePlaneLifeBitmap", bluePlaneLifeBitmap);

        this.setContentView(new GameView(MainActivity.this, "1"));

    }
}
```

Mediator Pattern Game

Mediator Pattern : Defines simplified communication between classes. Define an object that encapsulates how a set of objects interact. Mediator promotes loose coupling by keeping objects from referring to each other explicitly, and it lets you vary their interaction independently.

```
Bullet bullet = bulletList.get(j);
if (bullet.collideWith(enemyPlane)) {
    enemyPlane.setVisible(false);
    bullet.setVisible(false);
    mediator.handle(canvas, enemyPlane.getX(), enemyPlane.getY());

    ObserverData data = new ObserverData();
    data.setNotifyType(NotifyType.INCREMENT_SCORE);
    data.setScore(100);
    plane.notifyAll(data);
}

if (plane.collideWith(enemyPlane)) {
    enemyPlane.setVisible(false);
    mediator.handle(canvas, enemyPlane.getX(), enemyPlane.getY());
```

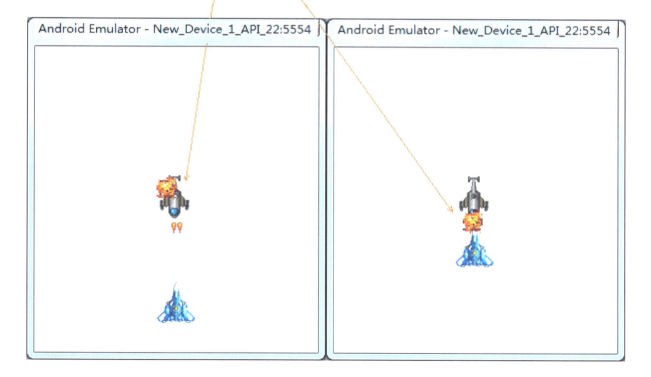

109

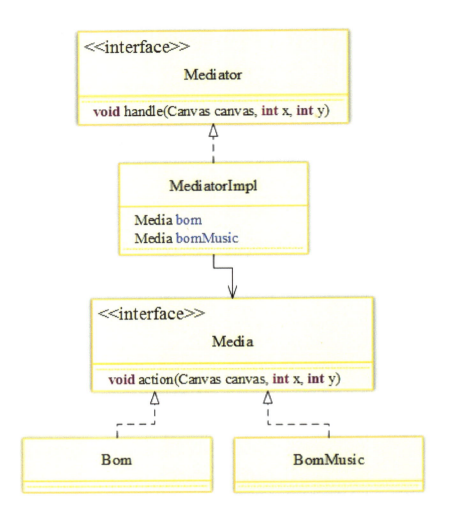

Copy all previous chapter chain pattern, Observer pattern code here

Media.java

```java
package com.vere.game;

import android.graphics.Canvas;

public interface Media {

    public void action(Canvas canvas, int x, int y);
}
```

Bom.java

```java
package com.vere.game;

import android.graphics.Canvas;

public class Bom extends Sprite implements Media
{
    public Bom() {
        super(ImageCache.get("bomBitmap"),0, 0);
    }

    @Override
    public void action(Canvas canvas, int x, int y) {
        this.setVisible(true);
        this.x = x;
        this.y = y;
        super.draw(canvas);
        this.setVisible(false);
    }
}
```

Create res->raw and then Copy hit.wav to this raw directory

```
▼  🗎 res                          9
  ▶  📁 drawable           10  public BomMusic(Context context){
  ▶  📁 layout             11      this.context=context;
  ▶  📁 mipmap             12      player=MediaPlayer.create(context, R.raw.hit);
  ▼  📁 raw                13  }
       🎵 hit.wav          14
  ▶  📁 values             15
                           16
```

BomMusic.java

```java
package com.vere.game;

import android.content.Context;
import android.graphics.Canvas;
import android.media.MediaPlayer;

public class BomMusic implements Runnable, Media {
    private MediaPlayer player;
    private Context context;

    public BomMusic(Context context){
        this.context=context;
        player=MediaPlayer.create(context, R.raw.hit);
    }

    public void run() {
        player.start();
    }

    @Override
    public void action(Canvas canvas, int x, int y) {
        new Thread(this).start();
    }
}
```

112

Mediator.java

```java
package com.vere.game;

import android.graphics.Canvas;

public interface Mediator {

    public void handle(Canvas canvas, int x, int y);
}
```

MediatorImpl.java

```java
package com.vere.game;

import android.content.Context;
import android.graphics.Canvas;

public class MediatorImpl implements Mediator{
    private Bom bom;
    private BomMusic bomMusic;

    public MediatorImpl(Context context){
        bom = new Bom();
        bomMusic = new BomMusic(context);
    }

    @Override
    public void handle(Canvas canvas, int x, int y){
        bom.action(canvas, x, y);
        bomMusic.action(canvas, x, y);
    }

}
```

GameView.java

```java
package com.vere.game;

import android.graphics.*;
import android.view.MotionEvent;
import android.view.SurfaceHolder;
import android.view.SurfaceView;

import java.util.List;
import java.util.concurrent.CopyOnWriteArrayList;

public class GameView extends SurfaceView implements Runnable, SurfaceHolder.Callback {
    private MainActivity gameActivity;
    private boolean isRun = true;
    private SurfaceHolder surfaceHolder;
    private Paint paint;
    private Plane plane;
    private int canvasWidth, canvasHeight;
    private int downX, downY;//coordinates of the mouse down
    private int moveX, moveY;//coordinates of the mouse move
    private String planeType;
    private EnemyPlaneChain enemyPlaneChain;
    private PlaneLife planeLife;
    private PlaneScore planeScore;
    private Mediator mediator ;

    public GameView(MainActivity gameActivity, String planeType) {
        super(gameActivity);
        this.gameActivity = gameActivity;
        this.planeType = planeType;

        surfaceHolder = this.getHolder();
        surfaceHolder.addCallback(this);
    }

    public void surfaceCreated(SurfaceHolder holder) {
        this.setFocusable(true);
        this.setFocusableInTouchMode(true);
        this.canvasWidth = this.getWidth(); // get width of canvas
        this.canvasHeight = this.getHeight(); // get height of canvas
        this.surfaceHolder = holder;
        paint = new Paint();

        //create plane SpriteFactory
        plane = PlaneFactory.create(this.planeType, 0, 0);
        plane.setX(this.canvasWidth / 2 - plane.getWidth() / 2);
        plane.setY(this.canvasHeight - plane.getHeight() - 40);
```

114

```java
    enemyPlaneChain = new EnemyPlaneChain();
    enemyPlaneChain.add(new Enemy1Handler(canvasWidth));
    enemyPlaneChain.add(new Enemy2Handler(canvasWidth));
    enemyPlaneChain.add(new EnemyBossHandler(canvasWidth));

    planeLife = new PlaneLife(0, 0, canvasWidth, canvasHeight);
    plane.registerObserver(planeLife);

    planeScore=new PlaneScore(0,0,canvasWidth,canvasHeight );
    plane.registerObserver(planeScore);

    mediator = new MediatorImpl(this.gameActivity);

    new Thread(this).start(); // start game loop thread
}

public void surfaceChanged(SurfaceHolder holder, int format, int width, int height) {

}

public void surfaceDestroyed(SurfaceHolder holder) {
    isRun = false;
}

@Override
public boolean onTouchEvent(MotionEvent event) {
    if (event.getAction() == MotionEvent.ACTION_DOWN) {
        downX = (int) event.getX();
        downY = (int) event.getY();
    } else if (event.getAction() == MotionEvent.ACTION_MOVE) {
        moveX = (int) event.getX();
        moveY = (int) event.getY();

        //Calculate the distance moved by the mouse
        int distanceX = moveX - downX;
        int distanceY = moveY - downY;

        if (plane.contains(downX, downY)) {
            //The plane follows the mouse move
            plane.move(distanceX, distanceY);
        }

        //Save moving coordinates to down coordinates
        downX = moveX;
        downY = moveY;
    }
    return true;
}
```

```java
public void drawGame(Canvas canvas) {
    canvas.drawColor(Color.WHITE);
    plane.draw(canvas); //draw plane on canvas

    plane.createBullets("2");
    plane.drawBullets(canvas);
    plane.moveBullet(0, -8);

    planeLife.draw(canvas);
    planeScore.draw(canvas, paint);

    enemyPlaneChain.moveEnemyPlanes(canvas);

    collideCheck(canvas);
}

private void collideCheck(Canvas canvas) {
    List<Sprite> enemyPlaneList = enemyPlaneChain.getEnemyPlaneList();
    CopyOnWriteArrayList<Bullet> bulletList = plane.getBulletList();
    for (int i = 0; i < enemyPlaneList.size(); i++) {
        Sprite enemyPlane = enemyPlaneList.get(i);
        for(int j=0; j<bulletList.size();j++) {
            Bullet bullet = bulletList.get(j);
            if (bullet.collideWith(enemyPlane)) {
                enemyPlane.setVisible(false);
                bullet.setVisible(false);
                mediator.handle(canvas, enemyPlane.getX(), enemyPlane.getY());

                ObserverData data = new ObserverData();
                data.setNotifyType(NotifyType.INCREMENT_SCORE);
                data.setScore(100);
                plane.notifyAll(data);
            }

            if (plane.collideWith(enemyPlane)) {
                enemyPlane.setVisible(false);
                mediator.handle(canvas, enemyPlane.getX(), enemyPlane.getY());

                ObserverData data = new ObserverData();
                data.setNotifyType(NotifyType.PLANE_DESTROTRY);
                plane.notifyAll(data);

                plane.setX(this.canvasWidth / 2 - plane.getWidth() / 2);
                plane.setY(this.canvasHeight - plane.getHeight() - 30);
            }
        }
    }
}
```

```
// game loop to repeat draw
public void run() {
   while (isRun) {
      Canvas canvas = null;
      try {
         canvas = surfaceHolder.lockCanvas();
         synchronized (surfaceHolder) {
            drawGame(canvas); // draw images of games
         }
         Thread.sleep(50);
      } catch (Exception e) {
         e.printStackTrace();
      } finally {
         if (canvas != null) {
            surfaceHolder.unlockCanvasAndPost(canvas);
         }
      }
   }
}
```

MainActivity.java

canvas.setFocusable(true): Set focus to activate keyboard events
canvas.requestFocus(): Set focus to activate keyboard events

```
package com.vere.game;

import androidx.appcompat.app.AppCompatActivity;

import android.app.AlertDialog;
import android.content.DialogInterface;
import android.graphics.Bitmap;
import android.graphics.BitmapFactory;
import android.os.Bundle;
import android.view.*;
import android.widget.ImageView;
import android.widget.Toast;

public class MainActivity extends AppCompatActivity {

   @Override
   protected void onCreate(Bundle savedInstanceState) {
      supportRequestWindowFeature(Window.FEATURE_NO_TITLE);
      getWindow().setFlags(WindowManager.LayoutParams.FLAG_FULLSCREEN,
WindowManager.LayoutParams.FLAG_FULLSCREEN);
      super.onCreate(savedInstanceState);
```

```java
        Bitmap bluePlaneBitmap = BitmapFactory.decodeResource(getResources(), R.drawable.blue_plane);
        ImageCache.put("bluePlaneBitmap", bluePlaneBitmap);
        Bitmap redPlaneBitmap = BitmapFactory.decodeResource(getResources(), R.drawable.red_plane);
        ImageCache.put("redPlaneBitmap", redPlaneBitmap);
        Bitmap redBulletBitmap = BitmapFactory.decodeResource(getResources(), R.drawable.red_bullet);
        ImageCache.put("redBulletBitmap", redBulletBitmap);
        Bitmap blueBulletBitmap = BitmapFactory.decodeResource(getResources(), R.drawable.blue_bullet);
        ImageCache.put("blueBulletBitmap", blueBulletBitmap);
        Bitmap enemyPlane1Bitmap = BitmapFactory.decodeResource(getResources(),
R.drawable.enemy_plane);
        ImageCache.put("enemyPlane1Bitmap", enemyPlane1Bitmap);
        Bitmap enemyPlane2Bitmap = BitmapFactory.decodeResource(getResources(),
R.drawable.enemy_plane2);
        ImageCache.put("enemyPlane2Bitmap", enemyPlane2Bitmap);
        Bitmap enemyBossBitmap = BitmapFactory.decodeResource(getResources(), R.drawable.boss);
        ImageCache.put("enemyBossBitmap", enemyBossBitmap);
        Bitmap bluePlaneLifeBitmap = BitmapFactory.decodeResource(getResources(),
R.drawable.blue_plane_small);
        ImageCache.put("bluePlaneLifeBitmap", bluePlaneLifeBitmap);
        Bitmap bomBitmap = BitmapFactory.decodeResource(getResources(), R.drawable.bom);
        ImageCache.put("bomBitmap", bomBitmap);

        this.setContentView(new GameView(MainActivity.this, "1"));

    }
}
```

State Pattern Game

State Pattern :

In a variety of states, a manager determines the different needs of the customer's needs in different states

1. Background scroll on canvas from one state to anther state

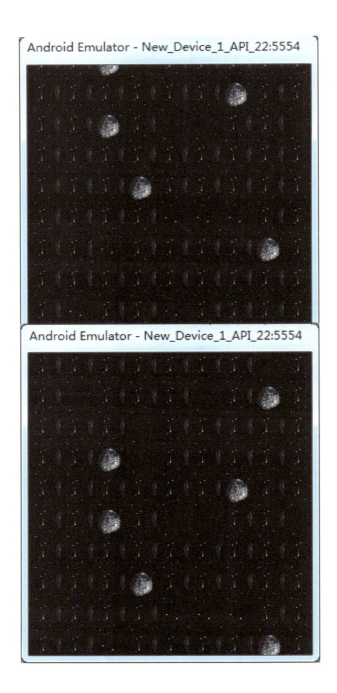

TiledLayer:

A TiledLayer is a visual element composed of a grid of cells that can be filled with a set of tile images. This class allows large virtual layers to be created without the need for an extremely large Image. This technique is commonly used in 2D gaming platforms to create very large scrolling backgrounds

Tiles:

The tiles used to fill the TiledLayer's cells are provided in a single Image object. The Image is broken up into a series of equally-sized tiles; the tile size is specified along with the Image. As shown in the figure below, the same tile set can be stored in several different arrangements depending on what is the most convenient for the game developer.

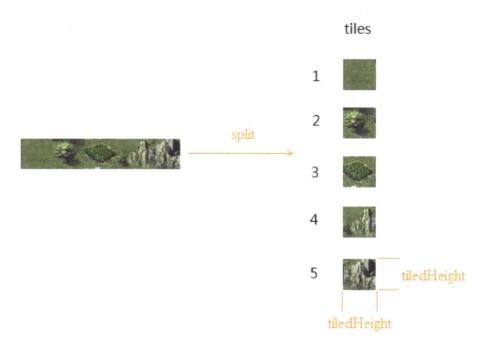

Each tile is assigned a unique index number. The tile located in the upper-left corner of the Image is assigned an index of 1. The remaining tiles are then numbered consecutively in row-major order (indices are assigned across the first row, then the second row, and so on).

Cells

The TiledLayer's grid is made up of equally sized cells; the number of rows and columns in the grid are specified in the constructor, and the physical size of the cells is defined by the size of the tiles. The contents of each cell is specified by means of a tile index;

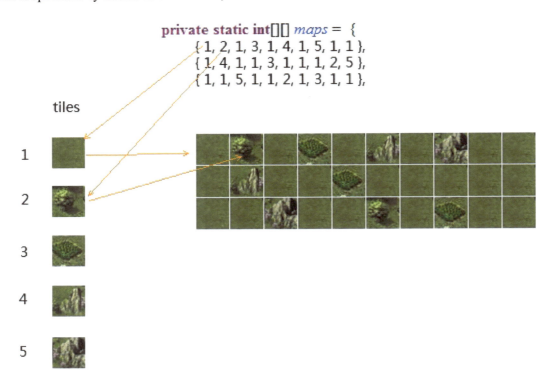

```
private static int[][] maps = {
    { 1, 2, 1, 3, 1, 4, 1, 5, 1, 1 },
    { 1, 4, 1, 1, 3, 1, 1, 1, 2, 5 },
    { 1, 1, 5, 1, 1, 2, 1, 3, 1, 1 },
```

tiles

1

2

3

4

5

```
private static int[][] maps = {
    { 1, 2, 1, 3, 1, 4, 1, 5, 1, 1 },
    { 1, 4, 1, 1, 3, 1, 1, 1, 2, 5 },
    { 1, 1, 5, 1, 1, 2, 1, 3, 1, 1 },
```

tiles

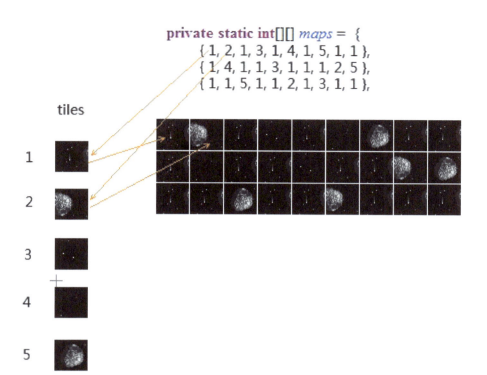

1

2

3

4

5

Use a two-dimensional array to clip the image into tiles and spread it on the background

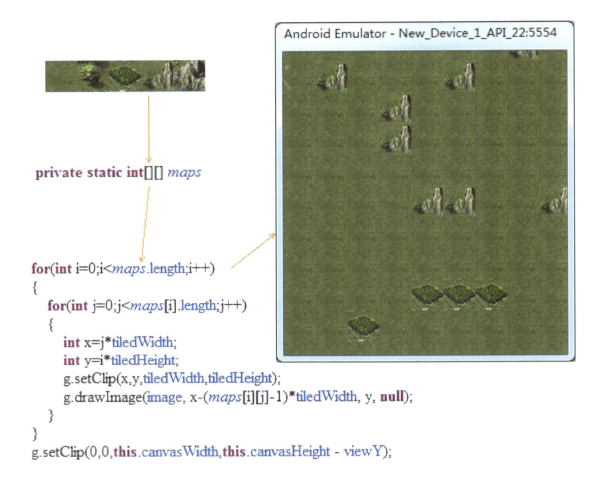

private static int[][] *maps*

```
for(int i=0;i<maps.length;i++)
{
    for(int j=0;j<maps[i].length;j++)
    {
        int x=j*tiledWidth;
        int y=i*tiledHeight;
        g.setClip(x,y,tiledWidth,tiledHeight);
        g.drawImage(image, x-(maps[i][j]-1)*tiledWidth, y, null);
    }
}
g.setClip(0,0,this.canvasWidth,this.canvasHeight - viewY);
```

Scrolling backgrounds:

translate(x, y): Translates the origin of the graphics context to the point (x, y) in the current coordinate system. Modifies this graphics context so that its new origin corresponds to the point (x, y) in this graphics context's original coordinate system.

viewY = -this.canvasHeight

canvas.translate(0,viewY)

viewY--

translate(0,viewY)

Scroll the backgrounds

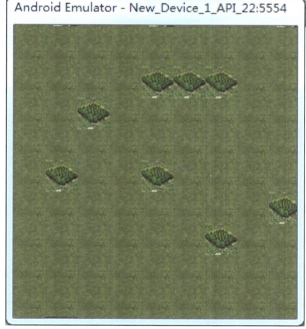

Android Emulator - New_Device_1_API_22:5554

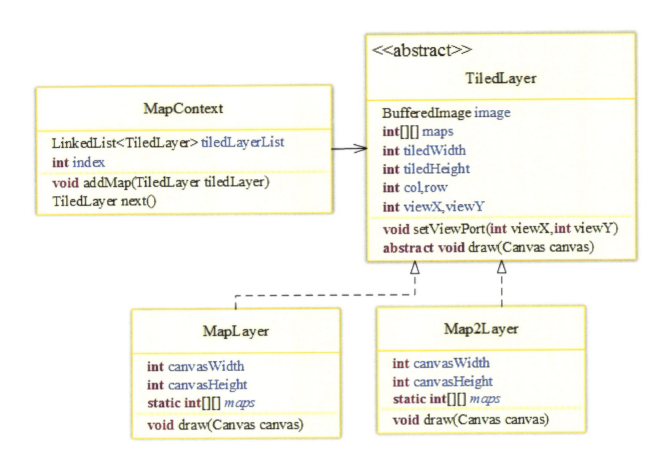

TiledLayer:

TiledLayer.java

```java
package com.vere.game;
import android.graphics.*;
public abstract class TiledLayer {
    protected Bitmap bitmap;
    protected int[][] maps;
    protected int tiledWidth;
    protected int tiledHeight;
    protected int col,row;
    protected int viewX,viewY;

    public TiledLayer(Bitmap bitmap, int[][] maps, int tiledWidth,int tiledHeight, int col, int row) {
        this.bitmap = bitmap;
        this.maps = maps;
        this.tiledWidth = tiledWidth;
        this.tiledHeight = tiledHeight;
        this.col = col;
        this.row = row;
    }

    public void setViewPort(int viewX,int viewY)
    {
        this.viewX=viewX;
        this.viewY=viewY;
    }

    public abstract void draw(Canvas canvas);

    public int[][] getMaps() {
        return maps;
    }
    public void setMaps(int[][] maps) {
        this.maps = maps;
    }
    public int getTiledWidth() {
        return tiledWidth;
    }
    public void setTiledWidth(int tiledWidth) {
        this.tiledWidth = tiledWidth;
    }
}
```

```java
    public int getTiledHeight() {
        return tiledHeight;
    }
    public void setTiledHeight(int tiledHeight) {
        this.tiledHeight = tiledHeight;
    }
    public int getCol() {
        return col;
    }
    public void setCol(int col) {
        this.col = col;
    }
    public int getRow() {
        return row;
    }
    public void setRow(int row) {
        this.row = row;
    }
}
```

ImageCache.java   **In the previous chapter**

ImageUtils.java

```java
package com.vere.game;

import android.graphics.Bitmap;
import android.graphics.Matrix;

public class ImageUtils{

    public static Bitmap scaleBitmap(Bitmap bitmap,int width,int height){
        int srcWidth=bitmap.getWidth();
        int srcHeight=bitmap.getHeight();
        float scaleWidth=(float)width/srcWidth;
        float scaleHeight=(float)height/srcHeight;
        Matrix matrix=new Matrix();
        matrix.postScale(scaleWidth, scaleHeight);

        return Bitmap.createBitmap(bitmap, 0, 0, srcWidth, srcHeight, matrix, true);
    }

}
```

```java
package com.vere.game;

import android.graphics.Canvas;
import android.graphics.Rect;

public class MapLayer extends TiledLayer {
    private int canvasWidth;
    private int canvasHeight;
    private static int[][] maps = {
        { 1, 1, 1, 1, 1, 1, 1, 1, 1, 1 },
        { 1, 5, 1, 1, 5, 1, 1, 1, 5, 5 },
        { 1, 1, 1, 1, 1, 1, 1, 1, 1, 1 },
        { 1, 1, 1, 1, 1, 1, 1, 1, 4, 1, 1 },
        { 1, 4, 1, 1, 1, 4, 1, 1, 1, 1 },
        { 1, 1, 1, 4, 1, 1, 1, 1, 1, 1 },
        { 1, 1, 1, 4, 1, 1, 1, 1, 1, 1 },
        { 1, 1, 1, 1, 1, 1, 1, 1, 1, 1 },
        { 1, 1, 1, 1, 4, 4, 1, 1, 4, 1 },
        { 1, 1, 1, 1, 1, 1, 1, 1, 1, 1 },
        { 1, 1, 1, 1, 1, 1, 1, 1, 1, 1 },
        { 1, 1, 1, 1, 3, 3, 3, 1, 1, 1 },
        { 1, 1, 3, 1, 1, 1, 1, 1, 1, 1 },
        { 1, 1, 1, 1, 1, 1, 1, 1, 1, 1 },
        { 1, 3, 1, 1, 3, 1, 1, 1, 1, 1 },
        { 1, 1, 1, 1, 1, 1, 1, 1, 3, 1 },
        { 1, 1, 1, 1, 1, 1, 3, 1, 1, 1 },
        { 1, 1, 1, 1, 1, 1, 1, 1, 1, 1 },
        { 1, 1, 1, 1, 1, 1, 1, 1, 1, 1 },
        { 1, 2, 1, 1, 1, 1, 1, 1, 1, 1 },
        { 1, 1, 1, 1, 2, 1, 1, 1, 2, 1 },
        { 1, 1, 1, 2, 1, 1, 1, 1, 1, 1 },
        { 1, 2, 1, 1, 1, 1, 2, 1, 1, 2 },
        { 1, 1, 1, 1, 1, 1, 1, 1, 1, 1 },
        { 1, 1, 1, 1, 1, 1, 1, 1, 1, 1 },
        { 1, 1, 1, 1, 1, 1, 1, 1, 1, 1 },
        { 1, 1, 1, 1, 1, 1, 1, 1, 1, 1 },
        { 1, 1, 1, 1, 1, 1, 1, 1, 1, 1 },
        { 1, 1, 1, 1, 1, 1, 1, 1, 1, 1 },
        { 1, 1, 1, 1, 1, 1, 1, 1, 1, 1 }
    };

    public MapLayer(int canvasWidth, int canvasHeight) {
        super(ImageCache.get("map1Bitmap"), maps, 216, 216, 10, 30);
        this.canvasWidth = canvasWidth;
        this.canvasHeight = canvasHeight;
    }
```

```java
public void draw(Canvas canvas) {
    for(int i=0;i<maps.length;i++)
    {
        for(int j=0;j<maps[i].length;j++)
        {
            int x=j*tiledWidth;
            int y=i*tiledHeight;
            canvas.save();
            canvas.translate(viewX, viewY);
            canvas.clipRect(new Rect(x,y,x+tiledWidth,y+tiledHeight));
            canvas.drawBitmap(bitmap, x-(maps[i][j]-1)*tiledWidth, y, null);
            canvas.restore();
        }
    }

}
```

```java
package com.vere.game;

import android.graphics.Canvas;
import android.graphics.Rect;

public class Map2Layer extends TiledLayer {
    private int canvasWidth;
    private int canvasHeight;
    private static int[][] maps = {
        { 1, 1, 1, 1, 1, 1, 1, 1, 1, 1 },
        { 1, 5, 1, 1, 5, 1, 1, 1, 5, 5 },
        { 1, 1, 1, 1, 1, 1, 1, 1, 1, 1 },
        { 1, 1, 1, 1, 1, 1, 1, 4, 1, 1 },
        { 1, 4, 1, 1, 1, 4, 1, 1, 1, 1 },
        { 1, 1, 1, 4, 1, 1, 1, 1, 1, 1 },
        { 1, 1, 1, 4, 1, 1, 1, 1, 1, 1 },
        { 1, 1, 1, 1, 1, 1, 1, 1, 1, 1 },
        { 1, 1, 1, 1, 4, 4, 1, 1, 4, 1 },
        { 1, 1, 1, 1, 1, 1, 1, 1, 1, 1 },
        { 1, 1, 1, 1, 1, 1, 1, 1, 1, 1 },
        { 1, 1, 1, 1, 3, 3, 3, 1, 1, 1 },
        { 1, 1, 3, 1, 1, 1, 1, 1, 1, 1 },
        { 1, 1, 1, 1, 1, 1, 1, 1, 1, 1 },
        { 1, 3, 1, 1, 3, 1, 1, 1, 1, 1 },
        { 1, 1, 1, 1, 1, 1, 1, 1, 3, 1 },
        { 1, 1, 1, 1, 1, 1, 3, 1, 1, 1 },
        { 1, 1, 1, 1, 1, 1, 1, 1, 1, 1 },
        { 1, 1, 1, 1, 1, 1, 1, 1, 1, 1 },
        { 1, 2, 1, 1, 1, 1, 1, 1, 1, 1 },
        { 1, 1, 1, 1, 2, 1, 1, 1, 2, 1 },
        { 1, 1, 1, 2, 1, 1, 1, 1, 1, 1 },
        { 1, 2, 1, 1, 1, 1, 2, 1, 1, 2 },
        { 1, 1, 1, 1, 1, 1, 1, 1, 1, 1 },
        { 1, 1, 1, 1, 1, 1, 1, 1, 1, 1 },
        { 1, 1, 1, 1, 1, 1, 1, 1, 1, 1 },
        { 1, 1, 1, 1, 1, 1, 1, 1, 1, 1 },
        { 1, 1, 1, 1, 1, 1, 1, 1, 1, 1 },
        { 1, 1, 1, 1, 1, 1, 1, 1, 1, 1 },
        { 1, 1, 1, 1, 1, 1, 1, 1, 1, 1 }
    };

    public Map2Layer(int canvasWidth, int canvasHeight) {
        super(ImageCache.get("map2Bitmap"), maps, 216, 216, 10, 30);
        this.canvasWidth = canvasWidth;
        this.canvasHeight = canvasHeight;
    }
```

```java
    public void draw(Canvas canvas) {
        for(int i=0;i<maps.length;i++)
        {
            for(int j=0;j<maps[i].length;j++)
            {
                int x=j*tiledWidth;
                int y=i*tiledHeight;
                canvas.save();
                canvas.translate(viewX, viewY);
                canvas.clipRect(new Rect(x,y,x+tiledWidth,y+tiledHeight));
                canvas.drawBitmap(bitmap, x-(maps[i][j]-1)*tiledWidth, y, null);
                canvas.restore();
            }
        }
    }

}
```

MapContext.java

```java
package com.vere.game;

import java.util.Iterator;
import java.util.LinkedList;

public class MapContext {
    private LinkedList<TiledLayer> tiledLayerList=new LinkedList<TiledLayer>();
    private int index;

    public MapContext(){
    }

    public void addMap(TiledLayer tiledLayer){
        tiledLayerList.add(tiledLayer);
    }

    public TiledLayer next(){
        if(index >= tiledLayerList.size())
        {
            index =0;
        }
        TiledLayer tiledLayer = tiledLayerList.get(index);
        index++;
        return tiledLayer;
    }
}
```

GameView.java

```java
package com.vere.game;
import android.graphics.*;
import android.view.MotionEvent;
import android.view.SurfaceHolder;
import android.view.SurfaceView;
import java.util.List;
import java.util.concurrent.CopyOnWriteArrayList;

public class GameView extends SurfaceView implements Runnable, SurfaceHolder.Callback {
    private MainActivity gameActivity;
    private boolean isRun = true;
    private SurfaceHolder surfaceHolder;
    private Paint paint;
    private int canvasWidth, canvasHeight;
    private TiledLayer mapLayer;
    private MapContext mapContext;
    private int screenY;

    public GameView(MainActivity gameActivity) {
        super(gameActivity);
        this.gameActivity = gameActivity;

        surfaceHolder = this.getHolder();
        surfaceHolder.addCallback(this);
    }

    public void surfaceCreated(SurfaceHolder holder) {
        this.setFocusable(true);
        this.setFocusableInTouchMode(true);
        this.canvasWidth = this.getWidth(); // get width of canvas
        this.canvasHeight = this.getHeight(); // get height of canvas
        this.surfaceHolder = holder;
        paint = new Paint();

        mapContext = new MapContext();
        mapContext.addMap(new MapLayer(this.canvasWidth,this.canvasHeight));
        mapContext.addMap(new Map2Layer(this.canvasWidth,this.canvasHeight));
        mapLayer = mapContext.next();

        screenY = -this.canvasHeight;

        new Thread(this).start(); // start game loop thread
    }
```

```java
public void surfaceChanged(SurfaceHolder holder, int format, int width, int height) {

}

public void surfaceDestroyed(SurfaceHolder holder) {
    isRun = false;
}


public void drawGame(Canvas canvas) {
    canvas.drawColor(Color.WHITE);
    drawMap(canvas);
}

public void drawMap(Canvas canvas)
{
    mapLayer.setViewPort(0, screenY);
    mapLayer.draw(canvas);
    if(screenY<=0){
        screenY++;
    }
    if(screenY>=0){
        screenY = - this.canvasHeight;
        mapLayer = mapContext.next();
    }
}

// game loop to repeat draw
public void run() {
    while (isRun) {
        Canvas canvas = null;
        try {
            canvas = surfaceHolder.lockCanvas();
            synchronized (surfaceHolder) {
                drawGame(canvas); // draw images of games
            }
            Thread.sleep(50);
        } catch (Exception e) {
            e.printStackTrace();
        } finally {
            if (canvas != null) {
                surfaceHolder.unlockCanvasAndPost(canvas);
            }
        }
    }
}
```

MainActivity.java

```java
package com.vere.game;

import androidx.appcompat.app.AppCompatActivity;

import android.app.AlertDialog;
import android.content.DialogInterface;
import android.graphics.Bitmap;
import android.graphics.BitmapFactory;
import android.os.Bundle;
import android.view.*;
import android.widget.ImageView;
import android.widget.Toast;

public class MainActivity extends AppCompatActivity {

    @Override
    protected void onCreate(Bundle savedInstanceState) {
        supportRequestWindowFeature(Window.FEATURE_NO_TITLE);
        getWindow().setFlags(WindowManager.LayoutParams.FLAG_FULLSCREEN,
WindowManager.LayoutParams.FLAG_FULLSCREEN);
        super.onCreate(savedInstanceState);

        Bitmap map1Bitmap = BitmapFactory.decodeResource(getResources(), R.drawable.map);
        map1Bitmap=ImageUtils.scaleBitmap(map1Bitmap, 1080, 216);
        ImageCache.put("map1Bitmap", map1Bitmap);

        Bitmap map2Bitmap = BitmapFactory.decodeResource(getResources(), R.drawable.map2);
        map2Bitmap=ImageUtils.scaleBitmap(map2Bitmap, 1080, 216);
        ImageCache.put("map2Bitmap", map2Bitmap);

        this.setContentView(new GameView(MainActivity.this));
    }
}
```

Thanks for learning

https://www.amazon.com/dp/B08HTXMXVY   https://www.amazon.com/dp/B086SPBJ87

https://www.amazon.com/dp/B08BWT6RCT

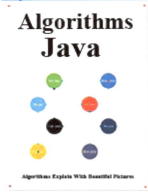

If you enjoyed this book and found some benefit in reading this, I'd like to hear from you and hope that you could take some time to post a review on Amazon. Your feedback and support will help us to greatly improve in future and make this book even better.

You can follow this link now.

http://www.amazon.com/review/create-review?&asin=B089CQK1YN

Different country reviews only need to modify the amazon domain name in the link:
www.amazon.co.uk
www.amazon.de
www.amazon.fr
www.amazon.es
www.amazon.it
www.amazon.ca
www.amazon.nl
www.amazon.in
www.amazon.co.jp
www.amazon.com.br
www.amazon.com.mx
www.amazon.com.au

I wish you all the best in your future success!